basic

Sampling

Printed in the United Kingdom by MPG Books Ltd, Bodmin

Published by SMT, an imprint of Sanctuary Publishing Limited, Sanctuary House, 45-53 Sinclair Road, London W14 0NS, United Kingdom

www.sanctuarypublishing.com

ISBN: 1-86074-477-X

basic
Sampling

Paul White

smt

Also by Paul White and available from Sanctuary Publishing:

Creative Recording 1 – Effects And Processors (second edition)
*Creative Recording 2 – Microphones, Acoustics, Soundproofing
   And Monitoring (second edition)*
Home Recording Made Easy (second edition)
EMERGENCY! First Aid For Home Recording
MIDI For The Technophobe (second edition)
Recording And Production Techniques (second edition)

Also by Paul White in this series:

basic Digital Recording
basic Effects And Processors
basic Home Studio Design
basic Live Sound
basic Mastering
basic Microphones
basic MIDI
basic Mixers
basic Mixing Techniques
basic Multitracking
basic VST Effects
basic VST Instruments

CONTENTS

INTRODUCTION

The sampler is perhaps the most widely used electronic instrument in contemporary music production and is employed across all musical styles, from dance to pop. When samplers were first developed, around a quarter of a century ago, they were hugely expensive, the sound quality was questionable and RAM (Random Access Memory) was so expensive that the total sampling time could be measured in seconds rather than minutes. Today, samplers are relatively cheap (there are even some freeware and shareware software samplers available on the internet), memory capacity is vastly greater and the software plug-in revolution has brought some interesting variations on the original hardware-sampler theme.

To the outsider, the sampler might seem like a mysterious and complicated instrument, giving the user almost unlimited powers to create and shape music, and in the right hands that's probably true. But there's no reason to be intimidated by sampling – the sampler is just another tool, albeit a very powerful one when used imaginatively. Most people appreciate that

basic Sampling

samplers can be used to record and replay sounds under the control of a musical keyboard, and one way of looking at a sampler is to think of it as just a different kind of synthesiser – one into which you can record your own sounds. For example, you could record or 'sample' a musician playing single notes on a violin, load those sounds into your sampler and then play those sounds at any pitch from a MIDI keyboard to create your own violin melodies or chordal string parts.

The other popular use of the sampler is to capture short musical phrases – often drum rhythms – which the user can then 'play' into his own compositions. Most dance tracks are built upon rhythmic loops, or repeating phrases, played back from a sampler, and in retrospect it's quite evident that the combination of sampling and MIDI sequencing is largely responsible for the dance-music revolution, as it makes the mechanics of producing this type of music relatively simple. That's not to say that compositional skill isn't required, however, because it will always be a requirement for the production of any form of music, but it does make the business of assembling musical parts from different sources relatively straightforward.

To use a sampler effectively, you need to know just a little about digital recording (because the sampling side of a sampler is really just a specialised type of digital-audio recorder), and if you're planning to use a MIDI sequencer then you'll need to know the basics of MIDI. Once the basics are out of the way, you'll know what your sampler can do for you and how to use it effectively.

This book covers both hardware and software samplers and looks at some creative ways in which samplers can be used, as well as covering the essentials of recording your own sampled instruments and drum loops. The first chapter deals with the basics of digital audio, including sample rates, bit depths and synchronisation issues. This area is particularly important, as many samplers include digital as well as analogue inputs and outputs, and there are certain rules that apply to digital recording that differ from those pertaining to analogue recording.

Meanwhile, Chapter 2 deals with the basics of MIDI and MIDI sequencing, simply because virtually all studio-based sampler use is associated with sequencing of one kind or another. If you're already familiar with digital recording and MIDI sequencing, you can probably skip the first two chapters and use them just for reference.

As with all of the books in this series, *basic Sampling* has been written with as little jargon as possible and

basic Sampling

with all of the necessary concepts explained in plain English. It covers all the essentials of using a sampler without being tied to any particular model or manufacturer and recognises the increasing popularity of software samplers. Additional sections cover creative sampling ideas, the use of library samples and issues relating to tempo-matching sample loops.

1 DIGITAL RECORDING

I apologise in advance for starting off this book with what seems like a rather academic subject, but the bottom line is that a sampler is a type of digital recorder, so in order to record sounds into it with the best possible quality you need to know a little background theory. Fortunately, the essentials of digital recording are reasonably straightforward and apply equally to other digital equipment in the average studio or live-sound rig.

All digital-audio equipment (and this applies as much to samplers as to multitrack recording systems) designed to accept analogue signals from microphones or other sources convert analogue input signals into a digital format that can be recorded and stored as binary information. In the case of a microphone, the voltage of the analogue signal produced by the microphone varies in proportion to changes in air pressure. A rapidly vibrating string, for example, will create equally rapid fluctuations in air pressure, which a microphone can then convert into variations in voltage. Because the signal voltage continually follows the variations in air pressure, the signal is said to be *analogue* – ie, the voltage is analogous to air pressure.

Digital systems use binary numbers – 1s and 0s – to measure voltages, and in the case of a signal from a microphone or other analogue source, the digital data measures the changing analogue voltage using just these two numbers, which are represented in the circuit by the presence or absence of a nominally fixed voltage. Converting an analogue signal into digital information involves measuring the analogue voltage at regular intervals and then turning these measurements into a sequence of these binary numbers. The process of performing this rapid succession of measurements is also known as sampling, which is potentially confusing in a book about samplers! In a digital-recording context, then, sampling relates to the way in which analogue signals are turned into digital signals.

As you might imagine, every second of sound needs to be sampled and measured many times if the end result is going to be an accurate rendition of the original analogue audio source. If you have enough instantaneous measurements per second, however, the original sound can be recreated accurately up to the highest frequency limit of human hearing. In fact, tens of thousands of samples must be taken each second if the original sound is to be reconstructed from the digital information with adequate accuracy.

Sampling Theory

OK, so the process of measuring and digitising tiny sections of the input signal is known as *sampling*, and audio needs to be sampled at very high rate. It's interesting to note that you need only around 25 frames of video or film per second to create the illusion of smooth movement, yet audio CDs employ a sample rate of over 44,000 samples per second in order to capture everything within the human hearing range, and just like film or video, each sample is a discrete measurement or snapshot taken at one point in time. The more often these measurements are made, the more accurately the curves of the original analogue signal are followed. Figure 1.1 shows what happens when a signal is sampled.

Sampling theory states that you must sample at a minimum of twice the frequency of the highest frequency you need to record if the output is to be reconstructed accurately. Frequencies above this limit must be removed before sampling takes place, or the data will produce ambiguous results and additional frequencies will be introduced based on the sum and

basic Sampling

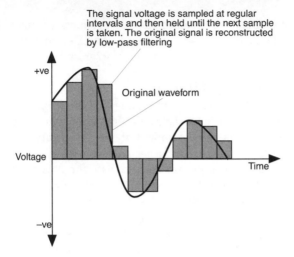

The signal voltage is sampled at regular intervals and then held until the next sample is taken. The original signal is reconstructed by low-pass filtering

Original waveform

+ve

Voltage

Time

−ve

Figure 1.1: Analogue-to-digital conversion

difference between the sampling frequency and the audio frequency. These frequencies were never present in the original signal and sound musically unpleasant.

The creation of unwanted frequencies by sampling at too low a rate is known as *aliasing*, and in order to prevent this it's essential to filter out any frequencies in the original signal that are above half the sampling frequency. Because no filter is perfect, the sampling rate must be made a little higher than twice the maximum audio frequency, which is why, for an audio bandwidth of 20kHz (generally agreed to be adequate for the reproduction of sounds audible by humans), the sampling frequency is 44.1kHz rather than 40kHz. If you're thinking that 44.1kHz is an odd kind of number (why not 45kHz or 50kHz?), you're right – as is so often the case, the reasons are historic in nature and irrelevant to the basic concepts. Other popularly used sample rates are 48kHz for broadcast audio and both 88.2kHz and 96kHz for high-definition audio, both of which can capture frequencies extend well beyond the range that can be perceived by typical humans. Interestingly, film and video can also exhibit aliasing effects, where the speed of movement captured is greater than twice the frame rate. This is most often evident when wheels on fast-moving vehicles appear to be turning in the wrong direction when the footage is played back.

The other major factor affecting audio quality is the accuracy with which individual samples are measured. Basically, the more digital bits that are used to represent each sample, the more accurate the measurement. CDs and DATs (Digital Audio Tapes) use 16-bit sampling, although most digital multitrack recorders and signal processors now use 24-bit conversion. In this context, more bits equates to less noise and lower levels of distortion. But why?

Digital numbers proceed in a step-wise progression – there are no halves or thirds of a bit – and the number of steps depends on the resolution of the analogue-to-digital (A-to-D) converter used in the process. Eight bits will give you only 28 steps, ie 256. This means that your loudest signal could have 256 steps but quieter ones would have considerably fewer. This gives a rather poor level of resolution and causes what's known as *quantisation distortion*, where the reconstructed signal differs from the analogue signal originally recorded.

Quantisation distortion sounds much like tape noise, the main difference being that it disappears in the complete absence of a signal, unlike most other sources of noise. Fortunately, using more bits gives a vast improvement in resolution, and most current digital processors convert to 16-, 20- or 24-bit resolution, with 16-bit resolution being the minimum for serious audio work.

One useful piece of information to remember is that each bit in a perfectly working sampling system equates to 6dB (decibels) of dynamic range, so an eight-bit system can give you a dynamic range of only 48dB at best. In other words, the loudest sound you can record without incurring distortion will be only 48dB louder than the background quantisation noise – ie, about as noisy as a cheap cassette recorder that doesn't use a noise-reduction system. In contrast, 16-bit resolution gives a maximum dynamic range of 96dB, which is hugely better. For even more impressive results, 24-bit systems can give practical dynamic ranges in excess of 130dB, but with these you have to balance this increase in specification against the quality of the sound you're recording in the first place – for example, if your source has a signal-to-noise ratio of, say, 70dB, which is likely for a typical microphone recording, it's arguable whether a 16-bit recording will sound any different to one taken at 24-bit resolution.

Some people say that digital recording is all about numbers, and that therefore all 16-bit digital systems sound the same as each other, but we now know that this isn't true. To obtain optimum accuracy, the numbers in digital data have to be recorded and replayed with exactly the same timing relationship if the result is to be accurate. This is where the quality of the converter and stability of the master timing clock affect performance – if the measurements are taken slightly early or slightly late, the recorded numbers are likely to be different than they would be if the samples were taken at exactly the right time. Clocking errors of this kind are known as *jitter*.

Levels

With analogue tape, you can push the signal levels into the red a little way before any distortion becomes evident. Indeed, this is a technique often used to create a warmer, more exciting rock 'n' roll sound on tape. However, digital systems work very differently, and they have no safety margin at all above odB. If you try to exceed this level, the signal will clip and probably sound dreadful, so when recording analogue sounds into your sampler, pay attention to your levels and get them as high as you can without allowing the peaks to clip.

Sample Rates

Simply stated, the sample rate is the number of times each second that an audio waveform is measured during the analogue-to-digital conversion process. This sampling must be done at precise intervals and is generally controlled by a very accurate crystal clock. Provided that the same sample rate is used for analogue-to-digital and digital-to-analogue conversion, the replayed audio will be of the same length and pitch as the original.

Although the minimum sample rate for serious audio work is 44.1kHz, less critical work is sometimes done at 32kHz, which reduces the audio bandwidth to under 15kHz, while broadcasters prefer to work with a 48kHz sample rate. Most DAT machines and soundcards support both 44.1kHz and 48kHz sample rates, but it's important to note that, where it's necessary to transfer a digital signal from one piece of equipment to another, both pieces of equipment must be set to run at the same sample rate and the sample clocks must be synchronised to each other. This is important because you may wish to record an audio sample from an audio CD directly into your sampler via the digital input. Even the very best analogue-to-digital converters introduce a small amount of signal degradation, so it's good practice to keep everything in the digital domain wherever possible.

Recent systems have been introduced that run at double the current standard sampling rates, so now 88.2kHz and 96kHz have been added to the list. In theory, these rates produce a slightly better sound quality, but in practice few people can detect a difference. My own view is that sample rates above 96kHz provide a sonic advantage only if the most esoteric equipment is used to make acoustic-instrument recordings in a very sophisticated studio. For pop- and dance-music creation,

I feel that they have little relevance. It's also important to appreciate the fact that the higher the sample rate you work at, the more storage space one second of audio requires. It's also true that the greater the bit depth (16 or 24 bits, for example), the more storage capacity is required, and with a sampler this means that the greater the bit depth, the shorter the playback time a given amount of RAM will provide. To cite an example, a 48kHz/16-bit signal takes only a sixth of the storage space of a 96kHz/24-bit signal, and yet in most cases the difference in sonic quality will be negligible.

The High-Sample-Rate Argument

The regular 44.1kHz sampling rate provides an audio bandwidth of 20kHz, which exceeds the hearing range of most humans, but there is a school of thought which suggests that recording with a much wider audio bandwidth will produce a better and more accurate sound, possibly because the anti-aliasing filters required at the analogue-to-digital (A-to-D) conversion stage can be made less severe and hence introduce fewer audible side-effects. The very steep filters used to block out everything above 20kHz in a 44.1kHz system can impart their own sonic signature to the sound, and even though designs have improved greatly in recent years, there may still be some audible artefacts generated by the filtering process.

The High-Bit-Depth Argument

On the face of it, it might be reasonable to suggest that, as current audio CDs use a 16-bit/44.1kHz format, there's nothing to be gained from recording at more than 16 bits. However, there are some valid reasons for recording at 24 bits, whether you're sampling or using a conventional multitrack recorder.

Whenever you process a digital signal by changing its level or adding EQ, it loses a little of its resolution due to errors incurred by the mathematical rounding up or down that takes place as the digital data undergoes multiplication or division. Furthermore, a 16-bit signal is at maximum resolution only when it's recorded at its maximum level. In this case, quieter sounds are recorded using fewer than 16 bits, so they always have correspondingly less resolution than high-level sounds recorded at the same bit depth. By recording and processing using more bits than you need for the final delivery medium (probably CD), you can preserve the maximum resolution possible right through to the end of the project. If, on the other hand, you record or sample everything at 16-bit resolution, your final mixed track might have a resolution equivalent to only 13 or 14 bits. Again, this is of little concern when dealing with pop music, which generally has a very limited dynamic range, but with acoustic music extremely quiet passages may end up being more noisy and more distorted than they need to be. In my experience, 16-bit sampling is fine for most 'normal' musical applications, but if you're working with music that has an unusually wide dynamic range, it may be worth exploring 24-bit sampling, so check whether or not you can hear a difference. In dance music, where sounds are often made deliberately lo-fi by processing or by adding vinyl noise, the benefits of recording at 24-bit resolution would seem to be outweighed by the benefits of recording at 16 bits and having a third more sampling time at your disposal.

Resampling

Some samplers have the ability to resample a sound that's already been loaded at a lower audio bandwidth in order to save on memory. For example, you might have sampled a bass-synth sound originally recorded at 48kHz, but because it has little or no high-frequency content you might decide that it sounds fine at a 32kHz sampling rate. In this case, you can resample or re-record the existing high-definition sample as a new sample at a lower sample rate and use that instead. Many hardware samplers include a resampling option, which may also be used to resample sounds to which onboard effects have been added. This has the benefit of freeing up those effects to be used in other ways.

Digital Connections

While you might never need to use a digital connection
with your sampler, they can provide a simple and high-
quality means of moving audio from CD into your
sampler. Unlike analogue systems, where every signal
needs to be sent down a separate cable, digital systems
allow two or more signals to be sent along the same
cable while staying completely separate, so you only
need one cable for a stereo signal. At this point, the
words *clocking* and *sync* need to be introduced, terms
which are equally relevant to hardware samplers,
computers, CD players, DAT machines and indeed any
other component of a digital-audio system.

Let's say you have a sampler with a digital input and
you want to transfer some musical phrases from a DAT
recorder or CD player into your sampler. The first step
is to connect the digital output from your DAT machine
or CD player (probably an S/PDIF phono connector) to
the digital input of your sampler. (S/PDIF is a standard
connection protocol developed by Sony and Philips
for consumer digital equipment, and on some
equipment it may be provided as an optical port as
an alternative, or in addition, to the phono co-axial
connector. Commercial-format adaptors are now
available for converting co-axial S/PDIF to optical and
vice versa.) On professional equipment, the digital

interface may be a balanced XLR connector carrying the AES/EBU-format signal, but the principle is exactly the same.

Now comes the clocking part. When you play the DAT machine or CD, a highly accurate crystal clock controls the rate at which the samples of data are played back, so for these little slices of data to get into another piece of digital equipment, the receiving device's sampling clock has to be running at exactly the same rate as that of the source machine. If the two devices are allowed to run independently, their clocks will always run at slightly different speeds (even if they're both set to the same frequency), resulting in clicks and crackles in the audio as the two clocks drift in and out of sync with each other. How to synchronise the two devices will be revealed shortly, but first here's a little more important theory.

Although digital coaxial S/PDIF connections use the same type of phono connector as audio cables, it's important to use a proper digital cable if problems are to be avoided. Conventional audio phono cables often appear to work fine, but the problem is that they're the wrong impedance and so don't provide accurate signal transmission. The result is an increase in error rate, even though you might not hear anything obviously wrong, as the receiving piece of equipment will mask minor mistakes via its own error-correction system. If the error rate gets too high, however, these errors can result in clicks or other audible glitches.

The reason why cheap audio cables don't work properly is because digital-audio data takes up a much greater bandwidth than analogue-audio data. At the high frequencies involved, impedance mismatches reflect some of the signal back along the cable, and these 'echoes' compromise the signal-to-noise ratio of the system to such a degree that, at some point, os may be misread as 1s, or vice versa. At best, the boundaries between 1s and os can become blurred, which introduces small timing errors – jitter. Using properly designed digital cable minimises reflections, however, and maintains the signal's integrity.

Both S/PDIF and AES/EBU carry a stereo signal plus a clock signal, but they operate at different voltage levels and so are not strictly speaking compatible (even though you can sometimes get away with using an adaptor lead between the two). AES/EBU is balanced (see Glossary), has a nominal level of 5v and can use conventional mic cables over short distances, whereas S/PDIF is an unbalanced 75-ohm system operating at around 0.5v, requiring digital 75-ohm co-axial cable.

Note that some S/PDIF connections use optical TOSLINK connectors, where the data is transmitted over fibre-optic cables rather than as electrical signals. The Alesis ADAT eight-channel optical format uses the same type of connector, so it's important not to get the two types mixed up. Also, both systems use the same types of transmitting and receiving devices, although their data formats are very different. No damage will be done if you try to connect an ADAT interface to one that uses S/PDIF or vice versa, but no signal transmission will take place either.

Clock Sync

The digital data carried along an S/PDIF cable also carries an embedded clock signal from the first machine, and this may be used to synchronise the clock in the receiving device. However, the receiving device must be placed into Digital Sync mode for this to happen. Figure 1.2 shows a DAT machine feeding to the input of a soundcard – just one way of getting digital audio into a software sampler. Most devices without such a Word Clock input facility switch to Digital Sync mode automatically if you switch them to Digital Input, but it's wise to check, as there are some exceptions – for example, some computer audio systems require you to select Digital Sync mode manually. The rule is that the source device runs from its own clock (Internal Sync mode) and the receiving device is set to Digital Sync.

Source of digital audio data – for example,
a DAT machine (master)

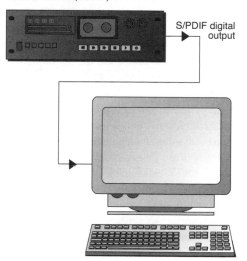

S/PDIF digital
output

Destination to which digital-audio data is being sent – for
example, a computer's S/PDIF digital input. In this case, the
computer would be the slave and so must be set to External
Digital Sync mode

Figure 1.2: Digital synchronisation

The main advantage of S/PDIF is that DAT IDs and CD
track IDs are carried as part of the data format, while
with AES/EBU they are stripped out. TOSLINK, the optical
version of S/PDIF, is also useful in situations where the

screen connector of a co-axial cable might cause ground-loop problems. On the other hand, AES/EBU ignores the SCMS (Serial Copycode Management System) copy-protection system used in some DAT machines to prevent cloned tapes from being recopied in the digital domain.

Word Clock
The majority of professional digital systems have a Word Clock facility, and this extends to some of the more up-market hardware samplers. With Word Clock, the sample clock is fed via separate sockets rather than relying on the clock embedded in the digital-audio signal. In complex setups, this can be more accurate and can mean that your system is less prone to suffering from clock corruption or problems with timing jitter. Word Clock usually travels via an unbalanced cable terminating in bayonet-fitting BNC connectors, and as with other digital interconnects it will normally be clearly labelled on the rear panel of the equipment. As with any other digital-clocking system, with Word Clock there can only be one master (in this case the master clock generator); all other pieces of gear act as slaves and lock to the master clock.

Using Word Clock has a number of advantages, not least being that you can avoid hooking up long daisy-chains of equipment. Long chains of this type can introduce clock instability as each piece of equipment tries to lock to the one before it, and in extreme cases this can result in either glitches or a total loss of sync. The other main advantage is that you can use a high-quality, low-jitter master clock to control everything, which should result in better audio performance.

Sample-Rate Converters

In situations where you want to work at one sample rate but some or all of the source material is at another, you'll need to convert these sample rates to the same value as the destination machine. (Note that, if you transfer the signals in the analogue domain, there is no problem with mixing source sample tracks.) In the studio, sample-rate conversion might be accomplished by an external hardware box, which will take in a digital signal at one sample rate and output it at another in real time, or it can be done in software – for example, if you have recordings made on a DAT machine at 48kHz and you wish to master a CD (which requires audio sampled at 44.1kHz), you'll need to convert the sample rate of the audio before you can compile the CD, or the final audio file will play back at the wrong speed.

Hardware samplers employ sample-rate conversion when resampling sounds at lower sample rates, but this is all quite transparent to the user. Similarly, plug-in software samplers automatically output data at the same rate as that of the host software, with no syncing problems, so in most respects these devices are easier to use than their hardware counterparts.

2 INTRODUCING MIDI

If you've already had some experience with MIDI, you might not need to read all of this chapter, but if you're coming from a more traditional recording background, it should help to get you up to speed without burdening you with unnecessary complexities. In the vast majority of situations, samplers are used in conjunction with a MIDI sequencer or via a MIDI keyboard, so a basic knowledge of MIDI is essential.

MIDI (Musical Instrument Digital Interface) can help the musician achieve a lot of things, some more obvious than others. MIDI isn't applicable only to keyboard players, but as the keyboard is the best-suited means of generating MIDI information, the majority of MIDI music is made using keyboards, so that's the format I'll use for this chapter.

MIDI can be used simply to connect different instruments, such as hooking up your hardware sampler to a MIDI keyboard, but in contemporary music composition the MIDI sequencer is central to everything, as it enables you to record all of the different musical parts of a composition a track at a time. You can listen to the various parts playing together at any time in perfect synchronicity, with each part playing back the synth or sampler sound of your choice. You can change these sounds after you've finished recording, change the tempo of your piece and try different musical arrangements by copying verses, choruses or phrases to other locations within a song.

MIDI Is Not Audio!

The reason why MIDI allows us to do all of these amazing things is because it isn't a system for transmitting sound; it's actually a system for transmitting instructions to devices (such as synths and samplers) that produce sounds. I like to use the analogy of a traditional musician writing a musical score that provides the instructions, while the player's instrument provides the sounds. MIDI works in the same way, except that MIDI's score is electronic in nature and the sounds are produced by electronic instruments. The original MIDI sequencer was a special type of multitrack recorder capable of recording not sound but MIDI information. However, current versions allow conventional audio tracks to be recorded alongside MIDI tracks. This makes it doubly important that you don't confuse audio and MIDI.

Whatever type of MIDI system you decide to use, you'll need a MIDI keyboard with at least a MIDI Out socket on the rear panel. Most have the full set of MIDI In, Out and Thru, which is necessary if the keyboard also produces sounds of its own. My advice would be to choose a keyboard that has something called *velocity sensitivity*. On these models, the harder you hit the keys, the louder the notes will be. Without this feature, all of the notes will be the same dynamic level, like a church organ. You might choose a 'dumb' master keyboard with no built-in sounds, or you might choose a conventional keyboard synthesiser with built-in sounds. And although sampling keyboards are available, the majority come either as rack-mounted units or as software plug-ins.

The MIDI Link

Linking MIDI instruments is accomplished by means of standard MIDI cables with five-pin DIN plugs on either end, available from most music shops. MIDI data itself is digital in nature – think of it as a sort of ultra-fast Morse code for machines.

The first thing to explain is precisely what musically useful information can be passed from one MIDI instrument or device to another via the MIDI cable. As this isn't a book dedicated to MIDI, I'll try to keep the explanation as simple as possible. The most important duty of MIDI is to tell the remote instrument what note to play, when to play it and when to stop playing it.

Anatomy Of A Note

When a key is depressed on a MIDI keyboard, a signal known as a Note On message is sent from the MIDI Out socket, along with a note number identifying the key being pressed. When the key is released, a Note Off message is sent. This is how the receiving MIDI instrument knows what note to play, when to play it and when to stop playing it. Up to 128 different notes can be handled by MIDI, with each key on the keyboard having its own note number.

The loudness of each note depends on how hard the key is hit, which is really the same thing as saying how fast the key is pushed down. This speed, or *velocity*, is read by circuitry within the keyboard and the data is used to control the volume of the sound being played.

The pitch of each note is determined by which key is pressed, although it's quite possible to transpose MIDI data before it reaches its destination. However, to keep things simple, let's assume that, unless otherwise stated, pressing a key results in the corresponding musical note being played by the receiving instrument.

MIDI Note Data

MIDI uses Pitch, Note On, Note Off and Velocity information to communicate to sound-generating devices how to play notes and which ones to play, and these messages all exist in the form of electronic signals. If the MIDI Out of the keyboard currently being played (called the *master* keyboard) is connected to the MIDI In socket of a second MIDI instrument (called the *slave*), then the slave is able to play the notes as performed on the master keyboard. This simple MIDI connection is shown in Figure 2.1. (Note, however, that, for this to work, both the master and slave must be set to the same MIDI channel, a concept that will be covered shortly.)

What Do These MIDI Sockets Do?

- **MIDI Out** – Sends information from a controlling MIDI device (master) to other MIDI devices that it is controlling (slaves).

- **MIDI In** – Receives MIDI information, which is then passed on to the MIDI Thru socket unchanged. However, if any of the incoming information is addressed to the instrument in question, it will

basic Sampling

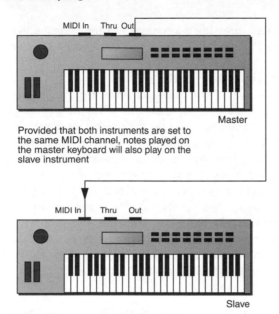

Provided that both instruments are set to the same MIDI channel, notes played on the master keyboard will also play on the slave instrument

Figure 2.1: MIDI master/slave setup

act on that MIDI data exactly as if it was being controlled directly from a keyboard.

- MIDI Thru – Sends a copy of the MIDI In signal, allowing several MIDI instruments to be linked together.

The Sound Module

The ability to link a second instrument via MIDI means that the sounds of both instruments can be played using just one keyboard, so the slave instrument doesn't need a keyboard at all. All of the playing is done from the master keyboard.

This leads nicely onto the subject of the *MIDI module*, which is simply a term used to describe the sound-generating and MIDI-interfacing electronics of a keyboard instrument packaged in a rather more compact (and generally less expensive) box. There's no reason why you shouldn't control multiple modules from a single master keyboard, but in order to appreciate the full implications of this you must first understand the concept of MIDI channels.

MIDI Channels

MIDI channels are the means by which certain messages are addressed so that they are recognised by certain instruments and ignored by others. In a typical master/slave MIDI system, the daisy-chain way in which the instruments are linked means that all slaves receive the same MIDI information. The MIDI channel system was devised in order to allow the master instrument to communicate with just one specific slave without all the others trying to play at the same time. The basic idea is that MIDI note messages are tagged with an invisible address label carrying their MIDI channel numbers. These messages are acted upon only when they are received by a MIDI instrument or device set to the same MIDI channel number. All other MIDI devices will ignore the message.

On a MIDI system, there are 16 channels, the idea being that MIDI information sent on channel 1 will be acted on only by slave instruments that are also set to receive on MIDI channel 1. The other modules still receive the information, but the MIDI data tells them that the data isn't on their channel, so they ignore it. By switching channels on the master keyboard, up to 16 different MIDI instruments set to 16 different channels can be addressed individually, even though they are all wired into the same system. The concept of MIDI channels becomes vitally important when you're dealing with MIDI sequencers, as they enable multiple musical parts to be played back at the same time.

Omni Mode Warning!

If a MIDI instrument is set to Omni mode (an option usually found in the 'MIDI Setup' menu), the system won't behave as you might expect. Most MIDI instruments can be set to receive on any of the 16 MIDI channels, but there is also a setting called Omni mode which allows a MIDI instrument to respond to all incoming data regardless of its channel. In other words, everything that comes along the MIDI cable is played. It's rather like having one member of an orchestra trying to play all parts of a score at once. For normal, 16-channel operation, instruments should be set to Poly mode. (The subject of modes is covered more fully later in the chapter.)

More About Modules

So far, I've described modules as being MIDI instruments in boxes but without keyboards attached, and this definition is true enough, as far as it goes. However, a great many modern modules – including samplers – actually contain several independent sound-generating sections, each of which can be addressed on a different MIDI channel.

These sound-generating sections are often known as *parts* because, in a typical system, each section can be made to play a separate musical part, and the ability to play multiple parts is known as *multitimbrality*. For example, a 16-part multitimbral module can play back up to 16 different musical sounds at once, each controlled via a different MIDI channel. For most purposes, you can visualise a multipart module as being analogous to several synthesisers sharing the same box. The same is true of most computer soundcards that have MIDI synth sections.

Multitimbrality

Like I said, modules capable of playing two or more different parts with different sounds are said to be multitimbral, although the individual parts share the same set of front-panel controls and some parameters may affect all voices globally. What's more, on low-cost modules and soundcards, the outputs from the various parts are usually mixed to stereo and then emerge via a single stereo pair of sockets. Also, modules often include effects sections, which must be shared between the parts in some way. However, you'll invariably find that you have independent control over which of the available sounds (or *patches*, as they're known in synth-speak) are selected, as well as the relative levels of the different voices, the left/right pan positions and the amount of effects – such as reverberation – added to each part, where available.

Similarly, drum machines are, in effect, MIDI modules with their own built-in sequencers allowing them to store and replay rhythm patterns and complex arrangements based on permutations of those patterns. The main difference between a standard synth patch and the way in which a drum machine organises its sounds is that a synthesiser tends to interpret incoming MIDI note data as different pitches of the same basic sound, whereas a drum machine produces a different drum, cymbal or other percussion sound for each MIDI note. Most multitimbral synthesiser modules and computer soundcards tend to have one part dedicated solely to drum sounds, so it's no longer essential to buy a separate drum machine unless you want to make use of the preset rhythm patterns that drum machines invariably provide. Samples of drum kits are organised in a similar way, enabling your sampler to function as a high-quality drum-sound module.

MIDI Thru Chains

The master instrument in a simple MIDI chain sends information from its MIDI Out socket to the MIDI In socket of the first slave. The MIDI Thru socket of the first slave is then connected to the MIDI In of the second slave, and its Thru is then connected to the MIDI In of the next one, and so on. The result is a *daisy chain*, and while in theory this can be indefinitely long, in practice this turns out to be untrue. What actually happens is that the MIDI signal deteriorates slightly as it passes through each instrument, and after it has gone through three or four instruments it can become unreliable, with notes getting stuck or refusing to play at all.

basic Sampling

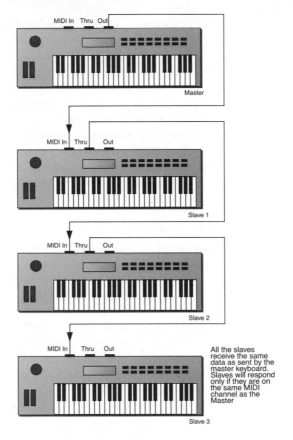

All the slaves receive the same data as sent by the master keyboard. Slaves will respond only if they are on the same MIDI channel as the Master

Figure 2.2: Daisy-chaining MIDI devices

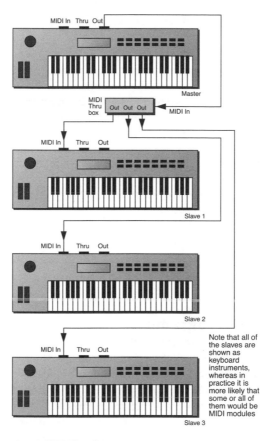

Note that all of the slaves are shown as keyboard instruments, whereas in practice it is more likely that some or all of them would be MIDI modules

Figure 2.3: MIDI Thru box

The best solution is to use a MIDI Thru box, which takes the MIDI Out from the master keyboard and splits it into several Thru connections, which then feed the individual modules directly. Figure 2.2 shows the standard method of daisy-chaining, while Figure 2.3 shows the same system wired using a MIDI Thru box. A MIDI Thru box simply splits a single MIDI signal several ways, although it also includes electronic buffering, as one MIDI source might not have enough power to drive several MIDI Ins at the same time.

Thru boxes can also be used in combination with limited daisy-chaining. If an instrument is fed from a Thru box, its own Thru socket may be linked to another module to form a short daisy chain. The only proviso is that these individual chains – each fed from one output of the Thru box – are no more than two or three devices long.

MIDI Programs

In the main, modern synthesisers are programmable, which means that they have the ability to remember many different sounds, each of which is identified by a patch or program number. New instruments inevitably come with some preset factory patches (which can't be changed) plus some space for users to store their own patches. MIDI can access directly up to 128 patches, sometimes numbered from 0 to 127 and sometimes from 1 to 128 – even standards aren't always all that standard! The buttons that are used to select the patches on the master keyboard also enable patch information to be transmitted to the slave synthesiser modules, enabling you not only to play the modules remotely, but also to select the sound or patch to which they're set. On some samplers, it's possible to select new patches by sending MIDI Program Change messages, but the necessary sound samples must already be loaded into the sampler for this to work.

Instruments that contain more than 128 patches must have these organised into two or more banks, each containing a maximum of 128 patches, because MIDI Program Change messages can access directly only 128 patches. However, there is also the MIDI Bank Change command, which is used to switch from one bank to another. MIDI banks are of more relevance when it comes to synthesisers than with samplers, but they're included here for reasons of completeness.

Continuous Controllers

In order to help the keyboard player imitate the expressive sound of a real instrument, a typical MIDI master keyboard has two or more performance wheels mounted to the left of the keyboard, and these are used to control pitch bend and depth of vibrato. Like the keys on the keyboard, these wheels generate MIDI information that can be used to control a slave module. Further control may be provided by means of a footswitch or pedal input – a sustain pedal, for example – that will allow a conventional volume pedal to be used as a means of varying MIDI control functions, such as level of filter frequency.

Because pedals and wheels can be set to any position, rather than simply being on or off, they are known as *continuous controllers*, although this name is somewhat misleading, as these 'continuous' controllers actually work in a series of small steps, with values from 0 to 127. MIDI controllers are important as they allow MIDI to convey more complex data than that signifying simply which note was played and patch-selection information.

MIDI Controller Data

The different devices with which a musical instrument may be controlled include performance wheels, joysticks, levers, pedals, footswitches, breath controllers and ribbon controllers, among others. You don't have to worry about MIDI channels or other technicalities when using controllers as the data automatically goes to the same destination (ie MIDI channel) as the notes you're playing on the keyboard.

Pitch-Bend Scaling

By changing parameters in their 'MIDI Setup' sections, MIDI instruments can often be scaled so that, for example, the maximum travel of the pitch-bend wheel might cause a shift in pitch of as little as a semitone or as much as a whole octave. However, if you want to use this technique, it's important to ensure that all instruments likely to play at the same time are set with the same scaling values, and this is especially true for pitch bend. Otherwise, when you try to bend a note on the master keyboard, the sound coming from the master instrument might go up by a third and the sound from the slave by a fourth! For general use, most people set up a pitch-bend range of two semitones so that a range of plus or minus one whole tone range is available from the centre position of the wheel. Most pitch-bend wheels are spring-loaded so that they automatically return to their neutral positions when released. You should be aware, however, that, although the pitch-bend wheel is involved in expression control, it doesn't form a part of the MIDI controllers group; for historical reasons, it exists in a category of its own.

More Controllers

On an instrument designed to work with the MIDI controller for master volume, turning up the master-volume slider on the master keyboard will send the appropriate control information (controller 7) over the MIDI system and the receiving synth will respond to it. A multitimbral module receiving a Master Volume control message will vary the volume of whichever part is being addressed according to the MIDI channel of the controller keyboard.

Another commonly used MIDI controller device is the sustain pedal, which operates rather like that on a piano by preventing the envelope of each note from entering its release phase until the pedal is released. A full listing of the controller numbers and their functions is included here for reference, as most samplers can make use of a limited number of MIDI controllers.

Controller Listing

0	Bank Select
1	Modulation Wheel
2	Breath Controller
3	Undefined
4	Foot Controller
5	Portamento Time
6	Data Entry
7	Main Volume
8	Balance
9	Undefined
10	Pan

11	Expression
12	Effect Control 1
13	Effect Control 2
14	Undefined
15	Undefined
16–19	General Purpose 1–4
20–31	Undefined
32–63	LSB for Control Changes 0–31 (where greater resolution is required)
64	Damper/Sustain Pedal
65	Portamento
66	Sostenuto
67	Soft Pedal
68	Legato Footswitch
69	Hold 2
70	Sound Variation/Exciter
71	Harmonic Content/Compressor
72	Release Time/Distortion
73	Attack Time/Equaliser
74	Brightness/Expander (Gate)
75	Undefined/Reverb
76	Undefined/Delay
77	Undefined/Pitch Transpose
78	Undefined/Flange-Chorus
79	Undefined/Special Effect
80–3	General Purpose 5–8
84	Portamento Control

85–90	Undefined
91	Effect Depth (Effect 1)
92	Tremolo Depth (Effect 2)
93	Chorus Depth (Effect 3)
94	Celeste Depth (Effect 4)
95	Phaser Depth (Effect 5)
96	Data Increment
97	Data Decrement
98	Non-Registered Parameter Number LSB
99	Non-Registered Parameter Number MSB
100	Registered Parameter Number LSB
101	Registered Parameter Number MSB
102–19	Undefined
120	All Sound Off
121	Reset All Controllers
122	Local Control
123	All Notes Off
124	Omni Mode Off
125	Omni Mode On
126	Mono Mode On
127	Poly Mode On

However, not all MIDI controllers deal with performance control. In addition to the last four controller numbers listed here, which change MIDI modes rather than note parameters, there are also Bank Change messages, an All Notes Off message (to cut off all notes that might still be playing), Local On/Off messages and a Reset All Controllers message, which causes all controller values to be reset to their default values.

The initials MSB and LSB stand for Most Significant Byte and Least Significant Byte, which is computer-speak for coarse and fine values, roughly speaking. Both MSBs and LSBs have a possible numerical range of 0–127, with variable controllers having values of between 0 and 127 and switched controllers usually set at 0 for off and 127 for on, although most modern instruments will also accept any value of 64 and above as on and any below 64 as off. Pitch-bend information can provide control in two directions, so its default position is midway between the two extremes, at 64. Your sequencer will take care of most of the obscure MIDI dialogue that takes place between your keyboard and you sound modules for you, but when you eventually come to edit the MIDI sequence data itself, it's always helpful to know exactly what the more common controllers and their respective values mean.

MIDI Modes

Instruments should generally be set to Poly mode for conventional operation, although some older instruments default to Omni mode every time they're switched on. Because the vast majority of work is done

basic Sampling

using Poly mode, most users rarely give MIDI modes a
second thought, but there are actually four different
MIDI modes, defined as follows:

- **Mode 1: Omni On/Poly** – The instrument will play
  polyphonically but will ignore MIDI channel data.
  Whatever you send it, on whatever channel, it will
  play. Some older instruments still default to Omni
  mode when they're powered up and so must be
  switched back to Omni Off mode before use.

- **Mode 2: Omni On/Mono** – The monophonic
  equivalent of mode 1. Hardly ever used.

- **Mode 3: Omni Off/Poly** – Often abbreviated to 'Poly
  mode', this is the standard MIDI mode, especially
  when it comes to sequencing or multitimbral
  operation. In mode 3, the instrument responds only
  to messages on its own MIDI channel and plays
  polyphonically.

- **Mode 4: Omni Off/Mono** – The monophonic
  equivalent of mode 3. Mode 4 is mainly for MIDI
  guitar players who need to have each string working
  on a separate MIDI channel in order to be able to
  bend notes or apply vibrato on independent strings.
  Because each string of a guitar is monophonic (ie

it can play only one note at a time), it makes sense
to use the receiving synth in mode 4 to mimic the
way in which a real guitar plays.

Non-Registered Parameters

Because not all synthesisers use the same method of
synthesis, it would be impossible to provide a standard
range of controllers able to access every parameter that
had an influence over the sound being produced. Some
parameters are common to all instruments, and these
are known as *registered parameters*, but in order to
allow manufacturers to provide access to the relevant
parameters of different instruments, the NRPN (Non-
Registered Parameter Number) system was added to
the MIDI specification.

The registered parameters are Pitch-Bend Sensitivity,
Fine Tuning, Coarse Tuning, Change Tuning Program
and Change Tuning Bank. However, the vast majority
of controls are non-registered, but for precisely this
reason it's usually necessary to have some form of
customised hardware interface or editing software to
access them. Because they are non-defined, the typical
user has no means of knowing what they are unless
they are detailed in the MIDI specification at the back
of the instrument's user manual. NRPNs are mainly used
to provide access for software writers creating editor

programs, although the more sophisticated MIDI user might also be tempted to make use of them.

Aftertouch

Another source of performance-control information is Channel Aftertouch data, which is produced by some keyboards when you press hard on the keys. This works via a pressure sensor under the keyboard and sends out a great lump of MIDI data, so if you're not using the Aftertouch function on your master keyboard, I'd advise you to turn it off in order to minimise unnecessary MIDI traffic. Also, when you're working with a computer sequencer, unnecessary controller data takes up a lot of memory. Conventional aftertouch affects all of the notes being played, as there's just one pressure sensor under the keyboard, while a few exotic instruments have polyphonic aftertouch that works independently for each key, although these are quite rare and highly specialised. Polyphonic aftertouch can generate a vast amount of MIDI data and so must be used sparingly, but very few instruments support this facility.

Aftertouch can be assigned to a number of different criteria, such as brightness, loudness, depth of vibrato and so on, and it's a useful means of adding expression to a performance.

Sound Banks

Where a synthesiser module contains two or more banks of sounds, a MIDI Bank Change message (also a form of controller message, involving controller numbers 0 and 32) is then used to access the different banks. (Note that not all instruments use standard Bank Change messages, although the relevant controller values will be supplied in your MIDI instrument's handbook as part of its MIDI implementation table.)

Assignable Controls

MIDI keyboard instruments often allow you to assign which physical control device relates to a specific MIDI controller. In this case, the modulation wheel on your synth could be redirected to control something quite different, such as the amount of reverb or the brightness of the sound being played.

How much you want to get involved with the various controllers is up to you. At first, you'll probably be happy to use the pitch-bend and modulation wheels and the sustain pedal, but as you get more familiar with MIDI you might be attracted by the possibilities of using a sequencer to automate your performance by controlling levels, creating automated panning, changing effects and patches and so on. The encouraging thing about MIDI is that you can start off very simply, making music right from the outset, and then, as you get more comfortable with the concept, you can get more ambitious.

Channel Messages

Most of the MIDI messages discussed so far are accepted by the receiving device only if they're on the same channel as the sending device, which is why this type of message is called a *MIDI channel message*. MIDI Note Ons and Offs are channel messages, as are all other types of performance messages, including those relating to velocity, pitch bend, controllers, program changes and so on.

MIDI Clock

Unlike channel-specific messages, MIDI messages related to synchronisation and sequencer control have no channel address and so are received by all of the instruments in a MIDI system. Perhaps the most important of all these *system messages* is MIDI Clock.

MIDI Clock is a tempo-related timing code and comprises 96 electronic 'clocks' or ticks for each four-beat bar of music. You can't hear these ticks, but they're recognised by any drum machine or sequencer set to External MIDI Sync mode, enabling the slave machine to stay in sync with the master.

A practical use of MIDI Clock is in syncing up a drum machine to a sequencer. When set to External MIDI Sync mode, the slave machine will follow exactly the tempo generated by the master device.

Start, Stop And Continue

The slave device also needs to know when to start and stop, so MIDI also includes Start, Stop and Continue messages. However, these are only of any use if you start your master device from the beginning of the song. Otherwise, the slave won't know where it's supposed to start from. To get around this, the MIDI Song Position Pointer message was added to the MIDI specification.

Song Position Pointers

Fortunately, MIDI Song Position Pointers (SPPs) are quite transparent to the user. At the start of a sequence, a message is sent which tells the receiving device where to start from. As a result, the slave device can lock up almost instantaneously, even if a sequence is started halfway through.

MIDI Machine Control

There is also a MIDI protocol for controlling compatible tape machines and hard-disk recorders, and this is known as MMC (MIDI Machine Control). This protocol allows the user remote access to the main transport controls and record-status buttons of a multitrack recorder. This can be useful if your multitrack recorder is on the opposite side of the studio from your sequencer.

MIDI Limitations

MIDI might seem to be instantaneous in its operation, but by modern computer standards it's quite slow. What's more, it moves in single file – it is a serial system. This means that, when you play a chord, all of the Note On messages are sent sequentially, but because MIDI is still pretty quick compared to the resolution of human hearing, the notes appear to sound at the same time. However, if you were to try to play, say, 64 notes simultaneously, you'd probably hear the delay between the first and the last notes played.

In reality, the speed of MIDI is seldom a limitation when you're dealing only with notes, but if you're trying to replay a multipart MIDI sequence that also contains lots of controller information, you could end up with the MIDI equivalent of a traffic jam, resulting in timing errors. In practice, it's wise to use controllers only when necessary and to switch off your master keyboard's Aftertouch function whenever you don't need it. That said, the better sequencers give priority to MIDI note timing when traffic gets heavy, so timing problems are less likely to be audible.

Sysex Messages

Sysex (system-exclusive) messages are part of the MIDI
System message portfolio, but whereas the rest of MIDI
is pretty precisely defined, Sysex is provided so that
manufacturers can build instruments with different
facilities yet which still conform to the MIDI specification.
Rather than use the MIDI channel system for locating
their targets, each Sysex message contains an ID code
unique to the type of instrument for which it's intended.
Where two or more identical instruments are being used
in the same system, it is often possible to assign an
additional ID number of between 1 and 16 to each one
so that no two have the same ID. If they did, they'd
both try to respond to the same Sysex message.

In the main, Sysex messages allow those people who
write sound-editing software to gain access to all of
the sound-generating parameters of an instrument that
might need adjusting. The programming parameters of
analogue and digital synths tend to be quite different,
and so manufacturers need to be allowed to specify
exclusive codes in order to be able to access their
specific set of parameters, just as they provide NRPNs
(Non-Registered Parameter Numbers) to allow access
to certain unique parameters using MIDI controllers.

Because Sysex messages are recognised only by the

instrument type for which they are designed, there's no risk of your drum machine trying to interpret a message intended for one of your synths and getting its brains scrambled.

Patch Dumping

Only advanced MIDI users tend to have more than a passing association with MIDI Sysex data, but anyone can use it at a basic level for copying patches or banks of patches from a synth into a MIDI storage device, such as a sequencer or MIDI data filter. Here's briefly how it works.

Most modern MIDI instruments have a Sysex Dump facility tucked away in their MIDI configuration pages somewhere. To use this, essentially all you need to do is connect the MIDI Out of the instrument containing the data you want to dump to your sequencer's input, put the sequencer into Record mode and start the dump procedure. The Sysex data will be recorded in exactly the same way as MIDI notes. However, if you look in the Edit list of your sequencer to see what's there, you'll see what appears to be random data.

Sysex dump data usually takes several seconds to record, after which it can be played back into the instrument at any time to restore the patches you saved.

(It's advisable not to quantise the Sysex dump after recording or it might not work properly.)

Compatibility

Most new MIDI instruments support most of MIDI's features, but few of these features are actually compulsory. About the only thing you can take for granted is that a MIDI synth will send and receive MIDI Note data, although virtually all will accept MIDI Program Change messages and Velocity information. If a MIDI message is received by an instrument incapable of responding to that message, it will be ignored.

The back pages of your equipment manual should show a table of which MIDI facilities are supported, where 'o' shows that the facility is present and 'X' shows that it isn't. This is known as the *MIDI implementation table*, and it can be very informative.

MIDI Merge

If there is a need to split the same MIDI signal to two or more destinations, you can use either the Thru connectors fitted to your MIDI instruments or a MIDI Thru box, but merging two streams of MIDI data isn't quite so simple. MIDI data is quite complicated, so if you were try to join two MIDI cables with a Y-lead, the result would be a jumble of meaningless data. Instead,

basic Sampling

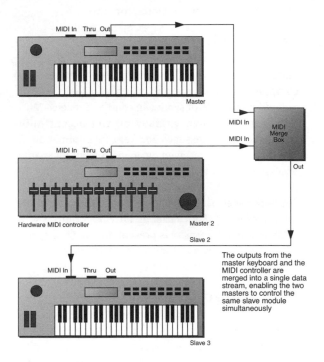

Figure 2.4: A basic MIDI Merge setup

a special device known as a MIDI Merge box is required. Figure 2.4 shows how a MIDI Merge box might be used to combine the MIDI outputs from a keyboard and from a dedicated sound-editing device, enabling both to be fed into a sequencer at the same time.

Merge facilities are needed when a sequencer needs to be controlled by a master keyboard while receiving MIDI sync signals at the same time, or when two keyboards need to be played into a sequencer at once. Any time that a MIDI device needs to be addressed from two places at the same time, a Merge facility is required. Most multiport MIDI interfaces include two or more mergeable inputs.

MIDI Sync

In a self-contained desktop-studio environment, synchronisation probably won't be an issue, but you'll still need to know something about the way in which MIDI handles sync if, for example, you need to lock your sequencer to another sequencer, a tape recorder or a video machine.

Tape Sync

The simplest MIDI sync system is FSK (Frequency Shift Keying), which records a series of electronic tones onto a spare track of the tape machine that will later provide the sync reference from the sequencer. The sync tones are related to tempo, and so the faster the tempo, the more sync pulses there are per second. A MIDI/Tape Sync box is needed to turn the MIDI Sync data from the sequencer into recordable tone bursts, and vice versa, although some drum machines have this facility built into them.

To synchronise a sequencer to tape (analogue or digital) using FSK, you must first program your entire drum part – complete with any tempo changes you might want to include – and then play back the piece while at the same time recording the sync-code output from the MIDI/Tape Sync box onto one track of your tape recorder. While recording the sync code, the sequencer's MIDI Out feeds the MIDI In of the MIDI/Tape Sync box and the Audio Out of the box is recorded to tape.

To run the sequencer in sync with the tape machine, the tape output from the sync track you've just recorded must be plugged into the Sync In socket on the MIDI/Tape Sync box and the tape must be started from the beginning. The sequencer should be set to External MIDI Sync mode, whereupon it will automatically start when it receives the sync code from the tape machine via the sync box, and it should stay in time with the tape until you stop the tape machine.

Basic FSK sync is simple, although it does have the problem that, whenever you stop the tape, you have to wind it right back to the beginning again in order to re-establish sync. Furthermore, unless your sequencer has more than one input with a MIDI Merge facility, you won't be able to record new parts onto the sequencer while you're locked to tape, because the sequencer's MIDI In will be taken up by the MIDI Out from the FSK Sync box. Of course, it's always possible to use a separate MIDI Merge box to combine the MIDI Out of your master keyboard with the MIDI Out of the FSK sync box.

Smart FSK

A refinement of the original FSK sync code, Smart FSK makes synchronisation easier, removing the need to always play the tape from the start in order to obtain sync. This refined system is designed to work with SPPs (MIDI Song Position Pointers) so that the tape machine can be started anywhere in the song and the sequencer will always find the right place. Fortunately, most modern MIDI equipment can generate and read Song Position Pointers.

Note that any of the above tape-sync procedures will work with a tapeless (or tape) digital recorder, but in most cases there's no need, as these invariably include the ability to output MTC (MIDI Time Code – see later) directly. The decline in the use of analogue tape recorders means that this method of synchronisation is becoming increasingly rare.

SMPTE

SMPTE is often used to synchronise a soundtrack with video footage or with other forms of professional system, and it's now supported by many MIDI interfaces and sequencer software. However, unlike Smart FSK, SMPTE is based on real time, measured in hours, minutes and seconds, with further subdivisions to accommodate individual frames of TV and film material. Because SMPTE is independent of tempo, a whole tape can be recorded or 'striped' with code before any recording or programming takes place.

SMPTE is available in a number of frame formats to accommodate TV and film, the most common of which are 24, 25 and 30fps (frames per second). Conversion from real time to tempo is carried out within the sequencer software, and most sequencers provide SMPTE support in a way that is very transparent to the user. The starting tempo of a piece of music and the location and details of any subsequent tempo changes are stored within the sequencer song file as a tempo map.

SMPTE stands for the Society of Motion Pictures and Television Engineers, the organisation that first developed it, although usually the term SMPTE/EBU is used to cover both US and European TV formats. American TV operates at almost 30 frames per second and film at 24fps, while European TV has a frame rate of 25fps. Apart from the more common 24, 25 and 30fps formats, the standard also includes *drop frame*, which is used for some specialist video-format conversions. The name of this system stems from the fact that whole frames are periodically discarded in order to eliminate cumulative timing errors. However, drop-frame time code is not generally used in audio-only applications.

Because individual frames of picture are too coarse a measure for audio work, additional resolution is gained by dividing individual frames into smaller units of time. MTC can be treated in exactly the same way as SMPTE, even though there are slight technical differences in the data format.

MTC

By far the most common synchronising system used in modern sequencers is MTC (MIDI Time Code), a MIDI-specific variation on the traditional SMPTE protocol offering the same choice of frame rates. Because MTC data comes in directly via your MIDI connection, the hardware requirements can be simpler, and most digital recording systems now output MTC directly, which means that no separate interfacing hardware is required. Where MTC is not directly supported by a digital recorder, third-party interface boxes are often available.

General MIDI

Most soundcards and many synthesisers include a bank of what are known as GM (General MIDI) sounds. These comprise a bank of 128 standard preset sounds that ensure nominal compatibility between instruments of different makes. General MIDI was a relatively late addition to the MIDI specification, but it's extremely useful as it allows writers to produce commercial MIDI files and be pretty sure of what types of sounds are going to be used to play back their compositions. This works because the sounds that are included in the GM sound set and their patch locations is tightly defined. This sound set includes a number of standard pop and classical sounds, as well as synth sounds and sound effects, and these are all located at the same patch numbers, regardless of the instrument or its manufacturer.

General MIDI is relevant only to those instruments bearing the GM logo. Furthermore, a GM machine might also be able to function as a non-GM machine, in which case it will have a dedicated GM mode or separate bank of GM sounds for those times when General MIDI operation is required.

General MIDI also includes drum sounds and specifies the keys to which the various sounds are mapped. Therefore, a bass-drum sound recorded on one GM-compatible machine will always play some kind of bass-drum sound on another, even if it doesn't sound exactly the same.

GM also specifies the minimum performance capability of each machine in terms of multitimbrality and polyphony. Essentially, the aim is to allow a MIDI sequence recorded using one GM instrument or sound module to be played back on any other GM device without the need to remap patches, move drum note allocations or worry about running out of parts or polyphony. This doesn't mean that all GM synths have to sound exactly the same, but it does mean that, for example, a piano preset on one machine must be in the same patch location as a similar-sounding piano preset on any other GM machine. In this way, commercial GM-format MIDI files or sequences from musicians with whom you might collaborate will always play correctly.

Although General MIDI applies mainly to synths, GM-compatible sound libraries are also available for samplers, enabling GM MIDI files to be replayed using high-quality sounds.

Polyphony And Multitimbrality

General MIDI instruments provide the ability to play back 16 parts on 16 MIDI channels, with a total polyphony of at least 24 notes. However, if you try to play more notes than an instrument can handle, you start to experience something known as 'note robbing', where previously played notes start to drop out. The whole idea of specifying a minimum level of polyphony is so that you don't run out of polyphony when trying to play a MIDI song file conforming to the General MIDI format.

Roland's GS format

Much of the present General MIDI format owes its existence to the protocols initially developed by Roland, who have since devised their own enhanced version of General MIDI, which they call GS. GS machines are still fully GM-compatible, but as well as the basic GM sounds they also offer several alternative banks of GM-type sounds to give the user more choice. The basic GM set occupies bank 0, with up to seven banks of variations on those original sounds. A Bank

Change command allows the user to switch between the various banks.

Yamaha also introduced their own expanded General MIDI format which they chose to call XG. Like Roland's GS mode, this builds on the basic General MIDI sound set, using several banks of alternative sounds. Most Yamaha XG instruments now also support Roland's enhanced GS format.

Basic GM Definitions

A standard General MIDI instrument must support 16-part multitimbrality, where the percussion sounds (of which there is a minimum set of 47) are on MIDI channel 10. These are mapped to keys in accordance with the General MIDI standard.

GM instruments must also be capable of 24-note polyphony or more, and notes are allocated dynamically. The specification allows eight notes to be reserved for percussion, leaving 16 for the other instruments.

All 128 preset sounds on a General MIDI device are defined by their type and patch locations, and all GM instruments respond to the same set of MIDI controllers and must also respond to Pitch Bend, Velocity and Aftertouch data.

General MIDI Voice Table

Prog No	Instrument	Prog No	Instrument
1	Acoustic Grand Piano	25	Acoustic Guitar
2	Bright Acoustic Piano	26	Acoustic Guitar
3	Electric Grand Piano	27	Electric Guitar (Jazz)
4	Honky-Tonk Piano	28	Electric Guitar
5	Electric Piano 1	29	Electric Guitar
6	Electric Piano 2	30	Overdriven Guitar
7	Harpsichord	31	Distortion Guitar
8	Clavichord (Nylon)	32	Guitar Harmonics
9	Celesta	33	Acoustic Bass
10	Glockenspiel (Steel)	34	Electric Bass (Finger)
11	Music Box	35	Electric Bass (Pick)
12	Vibraphone	36	Fretless Bass
13	Marimba (Clean)	37	Slap Bass 1
14	Xylophone	38	Slap Bass 2
15	Tubular Bells (Muted)	39	Synth Bass 1
16	Dulcimer	40	Synth Bass 2
17	Drawbar Organ	41	Violin
18	Percussive Organ	42	Viola
19	Rock Organ	43	Cello
20	Church Organ	44	Contrabass
21	Reed Organ	45	Tremolo Strings
22	Accordion	46	Pizzicato Strings
23	Harmonica	47	Orchestral Harp
24	Tango Accordion	48	Timpani

Prog No	Instrument	Prog No	Instrument
49	String Ensemble 1	74	Flute
50	String Ensemble 2	75	Recorder
51	Synth Strings 1	76	Pan Flute
52	Synth Strings 2	77	Blown Bottle
53	Choir Aahs	78	Shakuhachi
54	Voice Oohs	79	Whistle
55	Synth Voice	80	Ocarina
56	Orchestra Hit	81	Lead 1 (Square)
57	Trumpet	82	Lead 2 (Sawtooth)
58	Trombone	83	Lead 3 (Calliope)
59	Tuba	84	Lead 4 (Chiff)
60	Muted Trumpet	85	Lead 5 (Charang)
61	French Horn	86	Lead 6 (Voice)
62	Brass Section	87	Lead 7 (Fifths)
63	SynthBrass 1	88	Lead 8 (Bass & Lead)
64	SynthBrass 2	89	Pad 1 (New Age)
65	Soprano Sax	90	Pad 2 (Warm)
66	Alto Sax	91	Pad 3 (Polysynth)
67	Tenor Sax	92	Pad 4 (Choir)
68	Baritone Sax	93	Pad 5 (Bowed)
69	Oboe	94	Pad 6 (Metallic)
70	English Horn	95	Pad 7 (Halo)
71	Bassoon	96	Pad 8 (Sweep)
72	Clarinet	97	FX 1 (Rain)
73	Piccolo	98	FX 2 (Soundtrack)

basic Sampling

Prog No	Instrument	Prog No	Instrument
99	FX 3 (Crystal)	114	Agogo
100	FX 4 (Atmosphere)	115	Steel Drums
101	FX 5 (Brightness)	116	Woodblock
102	FX 6 (Goblins)	117	Taiko Drum
103	FX 7 (Echoes)	118	Melodic Tom
104	FX 8 (Sci-Fi)	119	Synth Drum
105	Sitar	120	Reverse Cymbal
106	Banjo	121	Guitar Fret Noise
107	Shamisen	122	Breath Noise
108	Koto	123	Seashore
109	Kalimba	124	Bird Tweet
110	Bagpipes	125	Telephone Ring
111	Fiddle	126	Helicopter
112	Shanai	127	Applause
113	Tinkle Bell	128	Gunshot

Note: Some manufacturers number their patches 0–127 rather than 1–128.

General MIDI Drum Map

Note No	Drum Sound	Note No	Drum Sound
35	Acoustic Bass Drum	38	Acoustic Snare
36	Bass Drum 1	39	Hand Clap
37	Side Stick	40	Electric Snare

Note No	Drum Sound	Note No	Drum Sound
41	Low Floor Tom	62	Mute Hi Conga
42	Closed Hi-Hat	63	Open Hi Conga
43	High Floor Tom	64	Low Conga
44	Pedal Hi-Hat	65	High Timbale
45	Low Tom	66	Low Timbale
46	Open Hi-Hat	67	High Agogo
47	Low Mid Tom	68	Low Agogo
48	High Mid Tom	69	Cabasa
49	Crash Cymbal	70	Maracas
50	High Tom	71	Short Whistle
51	Ride Cymbal 1	72	Long Whistle
52	Chinese Cymbal	73	Short Guiro
53	Ride Bell	74	Long Guiro
54	Tambourine	75	Claves
55	Splash Cymbal	76	High Woodblock
56	Cowbell	77	Low Woodblock
57	Crash Cymbal 2	78	Mute Cuica
58	Vibraslap	79	Open Cuica
59	Ride Cymbal 2	80	Mute Triangle
60	High Bongo	81	Open Triangle
61	Low Bongo		

MIDI Sequencers

Originally, all MIDI sequencers handled only MIDI – there was no audio capability – but then, some years later, fast computers and hard drives became affordable. Software plug-in samplers need an audio-capable sequencer in which to operate, but here I'll be focusing mainly on the MIDI aspect of sequencing.

A modern MIDI sequencer might more accurately be called a multitrack MIDI recorder, where the term *track* refers to a means of recording a musical part in such a way that it may be edited, erased or re-recorded independently of the other parts. Indeed, MIDI sequencing in general draws a close analogy with this way of working with multitrack tape, although the tracks contain MIDI data, not sound.

A typical MIDI sequencer will provide a bare minimum of 16 tracks and usually many more. Why more than 16 sequencer tracks might be necessary when there are only 16 MIDI channels will become evident shortly.

Music Layers

On a MIDI sequencer, you can record a number of separate musical parts at different times by playing the parts one at a time on a MIDI keyboard, by entering note and timing data manually or by a combination of 'live' playing and editing. The individual parts may be monophonic or they may comprise chords, while you could split a difficult part over two or more tracks set to the same MIDI channel and record them in several takes. Once you'd recorded them, you could then play these parts back via any MIDI-compatible instrument or collection of instruments.

Unless you use a hardware sequencer with a built-in synthesiser, you'll need one or more MIDI instruments to play back what you've recorded. These could be synthesisers or samplers and could be hardware modules or virtual-instrument plug-ins. The number of different musical parts you can play back at once is limited by the number and type of MIDI instruments you have. Fortunately, most modern synthesisers and PC soundcards are capable of playing back up to 16 different sounds at once, each controlled by a different MIDI channel. The number of software-synth/-sampler parts you can run at once depends largely on the power of the host computer and what other software is running at the same time.

Composing With MIDI

The MIDI composer usually records sections of music into the sequencer against an electronic metronome click set to the desired tempo. Tracks may be recorded in one take or tackled a few bars at a time, and the composition can be played back at any stage via a suitable synthesiser. When you're recording a track, you can assign any synth or sampler sound to it in order to hear what you're playing, and this sound will also be used for playback, unless you change it. However, if you aren't proficient enough to play the parts in real time, you can enter notes directly into the sequencer in much the same way as a composer would write notes onto manuscript paper. If you're not happy with something you've done, you can simply erase or change the unwanted notes, much as you'd correct a word-processor document.

The Sequencer Setup

In a typical setup, a master keyboard is connected to a sequencer via a MIDI cable, and when the sequencer is set to Record, any notes played on the keyboard are recorded as MIDI data into whichever sequencer track has been selected for recording. In a simple system, you might have 16 MIDI tracks set up so that each is on a different MIDI channel. Then, if you fed the MIDI output of the sequencer to a 16-part multitimbral module, you could play back all 16 tracks at once. Figure 2.5 shows a basic sequencing system.

If you have a keyboard that includes a synth, as shown in the diagram, simply select Local Off mode, which

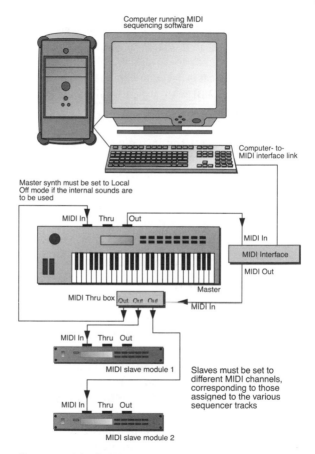

Figure 2.5: A basic MIDI sequencer system

isolates the synth's keyboard from its sound-generating circuitry so that, in effect, it behaves as if it was a separate dumb keyboard and MIDI synth module. Activating Local Off is necessary in order to prevent the formation of a MIDI loop, which would cause double or stuck notes.

Sequencers convert the incoming MIDI data to the appropriate channel for the track on which you're recording, regardless of the channel to which your master keyboard is set. This is known as *rechannelling*, and it means that, once you've completed recording one track, all you need to do is select the next one and play – you don't have to keep changing the MIDI channel on the master keyboard.

The Metronome

Although you could treat your sequencer as no more than a multitrack recorder for MIDI information, its real power lies in the way in which it allows you to modify and edit recorded data. When a recording is made, the sequencer is normally set to the tempo of the desired recording and a metronome click is generated. This means that the MIDI data is arranged in musically meaningful bars, which makes editing note timings or copying and moving sections of the MIDI recording much easier and more accurate than it would be if you switched off the metronome and played 'free'. For music incorporating tempo changes, it's generally possible to enter a new tempo at the appropriate bar and beat locations.

Where a rigid tempo is not appropriate, you can simply turn off the metronome click and play as you would when using a tape recorder. However, working in this way has the disadvantage that you can't use the sequencer's internal beat and bar structure to plan your edits, and you can't use the Quantise function, either, as the timing of your performance will be quite independent of the sequencer's internal tempo clock.

Quantisation

When a MIDI part is quantised, the timing is changed so that each recorded note is pushed to the nearest exact subdivision of a bar. For example, if you're working in 4/4 time and you select a value of 16 as your quantise setting, each note moves to the nearest point on an invisible grid dividing the bar into 16 equal intervals.

More sophisticated sequencers offer a Percentage Quantise function, which allows the notes you've played to be shifted towards the exact quantise division by a percentage. For example, if you set a 50 per cent quantise value, the note will be moved to a position halfway between its original location and the position of the nearest quantise division. This is great for tightening up your playing without losing all the feel.

Yet another quantise-related function is Swing, where the quantise grid is moved away from regularly spaced slots to alternating longer and shorter slots. This can be used subtly to add feel or more aggressively to turn a 4/4 track into a 2/4 track.

Tracks And Channels

A sequencer track is simply somewhere to record one layer of a composition, but the MIDI information recorded onto that track can then be sent on any MIDI channel you like. It's also possible to have several different tracks, all recording MIDI data set to the same channel. So why might you want to do this? Well, if you're recording a complicated drum part, you might want to put the bass and snare drums on one track, the cymbals and hi-hats on another and any tom fills on yet another. Not only does this make the parts easier to play, but it also makes it less confusing to edit them, should you want to make any changes. Figure 2.6 shows the Arrange page of a popular computer-based sequencing package depicting the layout of the tracks and the way in which recorded sequences are represented.

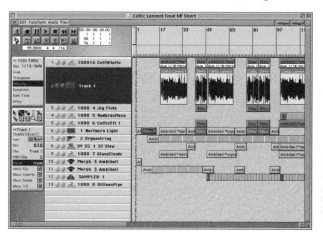

Figure 2.6: Sequencer Arrange page

Cut, Copy And Paste

Like a word processor, a MIDI sequencer allows you to move things around as well as delete or replace wrong characters – in this case, musical notes. For instance, if you want to use the same phrase or chorus more than once, you can copy it and paste copies of it into new locations so you don't have to record the same thing time and time again. Usually, copying is done graphically by dragging sections of a track with the computer mouse. Long sections can be broken up into smaller chunks using on-screen tools, such as Scissors.

basic Sampling

Unless you deliberately filter out certain types of MIDI data (some sequencers have the facility to do this), you'll find that your sequencer captures everything the master keyboard sends – Note On/Off, Velocity, Pitch Bend, Modulation and Aftertouch data, as well as other controller information and MIDI Program Change and Bank Change messages. This means that, if you change programs on your master keyboard halfway through recording a song, that Program Change message will be recorded and cause your synth to change patches each time the song is played back. If you find something weird happening, look in the Event Edit list and find out what's in there besides the Note data.

A sequencer track must also be told which synthesiser sound it's expected to control, and so, in addition to selecting the right MIDI channel, which tells it which instrument or part of a multitimbral instrument it is controlling, it's also necessary to enter the program number of the patch you want to hear. And if the synthesiser supports MIDI Bank Change messages, you also need to tell it which bank the sound is in. Some sequencers allow you to enter the patch names for the instruments that you've connected, which makes finding the right sounds easier. However, this doesn't apply to samplers, because they can play any sound you load into them.

When your MIDI sequence is played back, the sequencer transmits the MIDI information to the receiving synth in exactly the same order, and with the same timing, as it was originally played. With MIDI, though, you can change the tempo after recording without affecting the pitch, unlike on a tape recorder, where the pitch of the sound changes in relation to tape speed.

Sequence Editing

In the Edit pages of a typical sequencer, you can change the value, start time, length and velocity of any of the notes you've played, or you can build up compositions by entering the notes manually onto the quantise grid (or onto a conventional stave, if Score Editing is included) in non-real-time, rather like writing out music on manuscript paper.

Destructive And Non-Destructive Editing

Although quantising is irreversible on some budget sequencers and sequencing packages, all serious systems will allow you to unquantise something at a later time if required. In fact, many edits can be reversed because the original recorded data isn't actually changed at all – you only hear changes because the data is processed in real time as the sequence plays back. Such features are said to be *non-destructive*, as the original performance data is left intact. Even so, you should still save your work to disk regularly so that, if something does go wrong, you can go back to the previously saved version and pick things up from there.

There are often a number of related non-destructive editing options available, including the ability to transpose your music, either as you play or after recording; the ability to make the music louder or softer by adjusting the overall velocity; and the ability to use the same piece of data at different points within the same song. On some systems, you can even 'compress' the dynamic range of your MIDI data in order to even out the difference between your louder notes and the softer ones, in a manner roughly analogous to the way in which a hardware compressor treats audio signals. It may also be possible to delay or advance tracks relative to each other in order to change the feel of a piece of music.

Of course some edits are permanent, or *destructive*. For example, moving notes to new time locations or pitches and erasing or adding notes are destructive edits, as are cut-and-paste moves. Fortunately, like most programs, sequencers usually have an Undo function (indeed, some software has multiple levels of undo) that allows you to reverse the last edit you did, destructive or not.

The MIDI Interface

Most computer sequencers require either an external MIDI interface, a PC soundcard with a built-in MIDI interface or a synth module or keyboard with a built-in MIDI interface. For example, some keyboards and modules now come with a USB (Universal Serial Buss) connection so that they can be hooked directly to the computer – the MIDI interfacing is undertaken inside the keyboard or module.

MIDI interfaces for older Apple Macintosh machines plug into the rear modem or printer ports, while the newer breed of G3 iMacs and all G4s and above use the USB interface, as do most modern PCs. Also, PC soundcards dedicated to games usage will often include a MIDI interfacing facility, although it might be necessary to employ special adaptor cabling to make use of this. As a rule, if the manufacturer of your sequencing software also produces a MIDI interface, you'll be less likely to encounter compatibility problems should you choose to use it.

Multiport MIDI Interfaces

A basic MIDI interface provides a single MIDI output socket, which means that you're restricted to a maximum of 16 MIDI channels. However, you might want to use two or more multitimbral synthesisers to create a composition with more than 16 parts, or, as is more often the case, you might have several multitimbral synthesiser modules and want to change from one to the other without having to reconnect MIDI leads. The solution is to use a MIDI interface with multiple output ports – physically separate MIDI Outs that can each source 16 MIDI channels of MIDI data – which in effect make several different sets of 16 MIDI channels available at the same time. However, to use one of these, your sequencer software must also support multiple MIDI ports.

Within the sequencer, the ports may be designated by number or letter, giving you, for example, 16 channels on port A, another 16 on port B, a further 16 on port C and so on. (My sequencer, which uses a USB MIDI interface, identifies its ports as USB1, USB2 etc.) If a different 16-part multitimbral synth module is connected to each port of a four-port interface, you can use up to 64 different sound sources at the same time, each of which you can address individually by specifying its MIDI channel and port number. It's important to realise that you must buy a multiport interface that is supported by the sequencing software you choose. If you're a Mac user with pre-OS X operating system software, you may also need to use Opcode's OMS (Open MIDI System) or MOTU's FreeMIDI software to

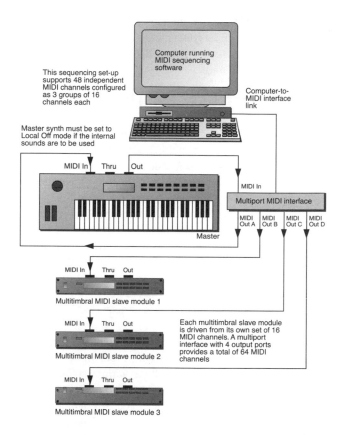

This sequencing set-up supports 48 independent MIDI channels configured as 3 groups of 16 channels each

Computer running MIDI sequencing software

Computer-to-MIDI interface link

Master synth must be set to Local Off mode if the internal sounds are to be used

MIDI In   Thru   Out

MIDI In

Multiport MIDI interface

MIDI Out A   MIDI Out B   MIDI Out C   MIDI Out D

Master

MIDI In   Thru   Out

Multitimbral MIDI slave module 1

MIDI In   Thru   Out

Each multitimbral slave module is driven from its own set of 16 MIDI channels. A multiport interface with 4 output ports provides a total of 64 MIDI channels

Multitimbral MIDI slave module 2

MIDI In   Thru   Out

Multitimbral MIDI slave module 3

Figure 2.7: A multiport MIDI interface

93

act as a link between your multiport interface and sequencer, which is generally supplied with products that need it. Figure 2.7 shows how a multiport system might be configured.

Sequencer User Interfaces

Most of the leading software sequencing packages have adopted the style of interface pioneered by Steinberg's Cubase, which uses a multitrack-tape analogy – the tracks are depicted as individual, stacked strips, with musical bars running from left to right across the screen. Once a section of a track has been recorded, it is shown as an individual stripe running from the Record Start location to the Record End location. This sequence may then be dragged (using the computer mouse) to a new position in the same track, or it may even be moved to a completely different track so that it plays back with a different sound. Blocks of sequence data may also be copied, split into shorter sections or deleted as required.

The main Arrange page (as shown in Figure 2.6) handles basic recording and arranging function, while further pages in the sequencer address various aspects of editing, scoring, audio recording, audio mixing and so on. The Edit pages usually allow you to examine (and change) the recorded data, either as a list of MIDI events, graphically as a 'piano roll' kind of grid display or as a

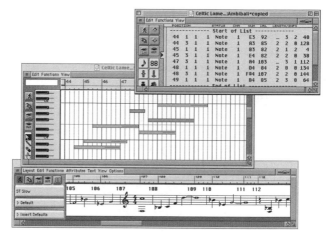

Figure 2.8: Common sequencer Edit pages

conventional musical score. Most sequencers also have graphical editing capabilities that allow you to manipulate controller information. Figure 2.8 shows some of the Edit pages from a popular software sequencer.

MIDI File Formats

MIDI sequence data tends to be stored in a file format specific to the software manufacturer, although some of the more popular sequencing packages allow you to transfer song data from one computer platform to

another and, in some cases, even from one
manufacturer's software sequencer to another's.

While there's no easy way of translating song files
between sequencers, you can instead save your work
as an SMF (Standard MIDI File) and transfer it that way.
SMFs were devised to allow complete interchangeability
between MIDI song files and also to make it possible
for third-party companies to provide commercial
sequencer files that can be read by any machine.
However, SMFs can handle only the basic 16 MIDI
channels, not multiport data, and they don't carry
information concerning any audio data or plug-in
settings that your sequencer might be using.

Most computers with floppy drives will read DOS-
formatted floppy disks, so if you're transferring MIDI
files from a Mac to a PC you must first format a disk
on the Mac in DOS format and then save your song as
an SMF. Then, to open the song in another sequencer,
use its 'MIDI File Import' facility, which is usually found
in the File menu. If you're using a more modern
computer with no floppy drive, you can still transfer
files as email attachments.

TIP: When emailing files to Mac users, it's always best
to use a suitable file-compression utility first, such as

WinZip or StuffIt, in order to preserve the file type (although Mac users can use a program such as FileTyper to reconstitute an individual file's creator). Data may also be transferred via CD-ROM, using 'Flash memory disks' (which are not actually disks at all), and I've even transferred files by using my USB digital camera as an external drive!

3 WHAT SAMPLERS DO

I find it easiest to visualise a typical sampler as a special kind of synthesiser into which you can record your own sounds rather than being forced to rely on a set of factory preset samples or waveforms. If you look at the block diagram of a typical sampler shown in Figure 3.1, you'll find that it bears a very close resemblance to the make-up of a simple synthesiser. The main difference is that here a sampled or recorded sound replaces the synth's oscillator.

Once a sound has been recorded into a sampler's memory – which uses the same type of RAM (Random Access Memory) as that used by desktop computers – it may be played back from a MIDI keyboard at any pitch, just like a conventional synthesiser patch. Even if you sample only one note from the original instrument, you can still play it back at different pitches, either monophonically or as chords – although, as you'll see later, there are limitations associated with the sounds that can be created from a single sample.

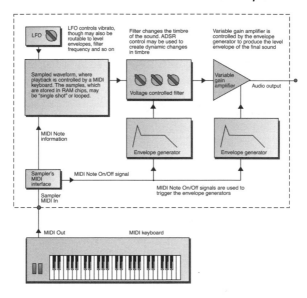

Figure 3.1: Block diagram of a sampler

Note also that there are simpler types of sampler known as *phrase samplers*. Essentially, these store and replay snippets of sounds without offering you the ability to change their pitches from a keyboard. Phrase samplers – which may be either stand-alone devices or built into some other product, such as a recording workstation – can be used to play a selection of individually triggerable musical riffs, drum loops and hits, sound effects or pretty much anything else that will fit into their memory. Playing is usually effected by hitting their trigger pads manually, or in some cases it may be carried out via MIDI. The main point to note is that such machines are very limited, compared to a full-featured sampler, and although they can be useful in the context of loop- and phrase-based music, they can't be used as a traditional, keyboard-playable musical instrument where the keys control the pitch of the note being played back.

In order for a sampled piece of audio to play back at a higher pitch than that at which it was recorded, it must be played back faster, and so doubling the playback speed will raise the pitch by one octave and cause the sound to play for only half as long as the original. If you slow down the sample in order to lower the pitch, the sound will correspondingly play for longer. If you've had any experience with samplers before, you'll have noticed that moving a sound too far from its original pitch can make it sound unnatural, and that some sounds suffer more noticeably from being pitch-shifted than others. For example, if you shift a human voice up by an octave, it sounds like an amusing (initially, at least!) cartoon voice, while dropping it by an octave makes it sound dark and demonic. On the other hand, a string sample can be shifted over quite a wide range and still sound reasonably natural.

Volatile Memory

Unlike the permanent ROM (Read Only Memory) -based sounds in synths, samplers store their sounds in RAM. This means that, when you turn off your sampler, you lose all of your sounds. Therefore, some additional form of permanent sound-storage facility is required, or you'd have to sample a new sound every time you switched on. Older samplers come with built-in floppy drives for this purpose, but a floppy disk is far too small for serious sampling work, so some other kind of removable-media drive or an additional hard drive is a must. Some samplers support these internally, like computers, while others use external drives that connect via SCSI (Small Computer System Interface) or some other common computer protocol. Unfortunately, the most common hardware samplers have their own floppy- and hard-disk formats, so you can't easily duplicate these floppies in your computer's own floppy drive or transfer your samples directly to your computer's hard drive. If you use only library sample CD-ROMs and don't make your own samples, you can get away with using just a CD-ROM drive from which to load your samples, but that would be to miss out on the fun of creating your own samples.

Sampling Applications

With the creative use of a sampler, even the most mundane sound can be transformed into something musically usable – for instance, by shifting it out of its usual pitch range or by applying other processes, such as modifying the loudness envelope or using synth-style filtering. Indeed, most of the sounds you hear reproduced in commercial synthesisers were originally created using samplers.

To make your sampled sound play back as chords, the sampler needs to work polyphonically, in the same way as a synthesiser, and just like any synth, there's a limit to the amount of polyphony you can have. With software samplers, you can usually set the maximum polyphony yourself. Remember, a lower polyphony setting usually equates to more efficient CPU usage, especially when using sounds with long release times.

While it's possible to sample a single sound and then play melody lines or chords based on just that one sample, more accurate-sounding results are obtained by sampling multiple notes from the original instrument so that you limit the range over which each note must be transposed. Pianos may benefit from having each of their notes sampled, while some other instrument sounds work just as well when sampled only once or twice per octave. This technique is known as *multisampling* and will be explained in more detail later in this chapter.

As RAM chips became bigger and cheaper, the available sample memory increased from mere seconds to tens of seconds, and then to minutes. Users soon discovered that, if they could sample individual notes from instruments, they could also sample entire musical phrases or whole bars of drum rhythms. The ability to sample complete musical phrases is fundamental to the composition of modern dance music, where the music is often built up from a series of drum loops. (Here, the term *loop* simply refers to a sampled section that can be repeated to form a continuous piece of music.) Most samplers will allow you to loop around any sound continuously, but with rhythmic samples this runs the risk of the loop gradually drifting out of time with whatever is recorded into the host sequencer due to minor variations in tempo between the sequenced and sampled parts.

With this in mind, in order to maintain perfect synchronisation, it's invariably better to trigger your rhythmic phrase once every bar (or whatever the length of the loop is) from your sequencer so as to keep the timing accurate. In this way, if the loop ends slightly before or after the end of the sequencer's bar subdivision, it will be retriggered at the start of the next bar, and so the error will have no time to build up to the point at which it becomes audible.

Memory Issues

So how much RAM should you fit to your sampler? This question applies both to hardware samplers, where additional memory is fitted into the machine itself, and to software samplers, where RAM is added to the host computer. The short answer is that you can never have too much sample memory, especially if you plan to use the instrument multitimbrally. A good figure to remember is that a mono sample lasting one minute will require about 5Mb of RAM at the CD sample rate of 44.1kHz. A minute may seem like a long time, but remember that stereo samples halve the available time, as do multisample sets. Also, if you use the sampler multitimbrally, the memory will have to hold several sounds at the same time, which further reduces the sample time available for individual sounds.

With multisampling, instruments tend to be sampled every few semitones in order to create a set of samples that sounds convincing over the entire range of the keyboard, and again this takes memory. Fortunately, RAM is now relatively cheap and most modern samplers let you add regular computer RAM rather than force you to buy expensive, proprietary memory boards. For this reason alone, it's worth filling your sampler to capacity as soon as possible. Computer users would be advised to add at least 256Mb of RAM over and above what they need to run the rest of their music software.

Even with a full complement of RAM, you may still find that you need more sampling time than you have available, especially when you're using long samples or sets of multisamples in a multitimbral context. If you can make do with a lower audio bandwidth, setting a lower sampling rate (or resampling an existing sample) will extend the time available to you, and by deliberately sampling at a very low sample rate, you can make sounds quite cheap and 'crunchy', a technique popular with writers of dance music. Meanwhile, users of soft samplers may prefer simply to 'write' a completed sampler part to a sequencer's audio track – with added plug-in effects, if necessary – as this frees up the CPU (Central Processing Unit) resources for that particular sampler part and any plug-ins that were used to process it.

Trimming

When you record a new sound into a sampler using a microphone, you might start the sampling process slightly before the sound starts. If so, you'll need to trim the start time of the sample so that the sound plays as soon as you strike a key. Similarly, you might have recorded a section of sound that's just too long, in which case you'd need to trim the end point. On most simple samplers, the sample-end point is the same as the loop-end point. (See the next section, 'Looping', for more details).

There are a number of hardware samplers available that have a sound-activated Record mode that will start recording once the sound level has reached a user-defined threshold. These devices can make capturing samples much easier, and this technique means that you don't have to trim the sample-start time, but be aware that you might lose the beginnings of slow-attack sounds, as recording will start only when the signal has risen above the trigger threshold.

Looping

Looping is a very important concept to understand in the context of sampling, and when you come to create your own samples you'll probably find that looping is the most difficult and time-consuming part of the process. Sustained musical sounds, such as strings or flutes, don't change character very much after their initial attack, so one way of lengthening these is to find a section of the sound that has a reasonably consistent character and then repeat it by looping it. In this way, instead of sampling the whole duration of the musical note, you simply sample the first few seconds and then use the sampler's editing facilities to create a loop, using material from the steady part of the note. This can obviously save a lot of memory, as well as allow played notes to be sustained indefinitely. Provided that the loop points are carefully chosen, you'll end up with a note that plays smoothly for as long as you hold down the key. However, if the loop points are poorly chosen, you'll hear a noticeable glitch or discontinuity as the sound repeats. Some samplers include auto-looping facilities that try to find suitable loop points for you, and by all means give these a try, but in my experience they work better on some sounds than others.

With most samplers that support basic looping, the looping sound will decay at a rate set by the sampler's Release control – activated when the key is released – just as a synthesiser would. As well as having the benefit of reducing the amount of RAM needed to play a sample, looping neatly gets around the issue of low notes being longer in duration than high notes due to the different playback speeds when a single sample is being used as the sound source. With a smoothly sustaining sound such as a flute or synth string patch, finding a suitable loop point is relatively easy, but not all sounds are so co-operative. In many cases, it's necessary to resort to crossfade looping. Figure 3.2 illustrates how a looped sound looks in graphical form and also shows a close-up of the waveforms at either side of the loop-edit point. These need to merge smoothly into each other if you want to avoid clicking, and so on a hardware sampler which will allow you to adjust Loop Start points in very small increments, it's worth making small adjustments in order to hear if the click gets louder or quieter. Make further adjustments in the direction that makes the click quieter until you find the point at which the click is least obvious. With some sounds, you might even be able to get the click to disappear completely, which means that the waveforms are in perfect alignment.

In reality, few real instruments are co-operative enough to produce a sample loop with a totally consistent level and character for very long, so you'll often find that the most carefully selected loop points are audible as changes in timbre, abrupt changes in level or clicks. Clicks are a real problem in situations where you can't get the audio waveforms on either side of a loop-edit point to match up, and some samplers have the ability to force edits to the nearest zero-crossing point (that part of a waveform where it crosses over from being

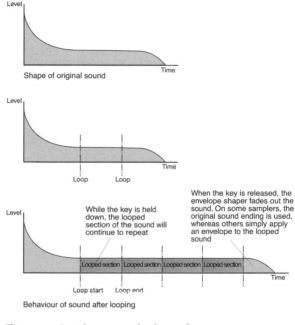

Level

Time

Shape of original sound

Level

Time

Loop   Loop

Level

When the key is released, the envelope shaper fades out the sound. On some samplers, the original sound ending is used, whereas others simply apply an envelope to the looped sound

While the key is held down, the looped section of the sound will continue to repeat

Looped section | Looped section | Looped section | Looped section

Time

Loop start   Loop end

Behaviour of sound after looping

Figure 3.2: Looping a sustained sound

positive to negative, or vice versa), which can help, but even this doesn't guarantee a click-free loop if the waveforms have very different shapes on either side of the edit. You also need to know that you haven't selected a zero-crossing point where the waveform goes from positive to negative at the start of the edit and negative to positive at the end, or you'll still hear a click. Not all auto-looping software is clever enough to pick zero-crossing points that cross in the same direction, so if yours doesn't get a good result the first time, just try it again.

Crossfade Looping

To help disguise audible loop-edit points, all serious samplers have a facility called *crossfade looping*. With this facility, instead of switching abruptly back to the start at the end of a loop, the sampler computes a gradual transition by fading out one end of the loop as the other fades in. The sampled data is then modified to reflect these changes and saved as a new version. (Note that, in some hardware samplers, this is a destructive process, so if you try a crossfade and it doesn't work out, you'll need to go back to the original sample and start again.) Unfortunately, some samplers actually change the original sample, rather than work on a copy, in which case it's advisable to make a copy of your sample before you experiment with crossfade looping. (In any event, you should always save your samples to disk before attempting to edit them.) Software samplers, on the other hand, tend not to change the original data but instead compute the crossfades in real time, as required. This has the advantage that you can revisit samples and make further adjustments to the loop-edit points and crossfade times if necessary.

Crossfade Lengths

A crossfade needs to be as short as possible, or the overlapping sound during the crossfade may appear unnatural, but at the same time it has to be long enough to hide any sudden changes. Hiding a click might require a crossfade time of only 20ms or so, whereas you might need a much longer fade time – typically hundreds of milliseconds – to hide a tonal discontinuity. Decaying sounds are often easier to loop if they're compressed (you can do this with a hardware compressor as you record the sounds, or by processing the audio using a software compressor plug-in after recording into an audio program), as this helps to keep the level consistent. If the level is consistent, at least you don't have to worry too much about level differences at either end of the loop.

Even using compression, you might find that the sound's own natural decay means that you still have a different level between the start and end of the loop, and even if you smoothe this out with a crossfade, you'll probably hear an unnatural modulation effect occurring at the rate that the loop takes to come around. What's more, as you play notes higher up the keyboard, the modulation rate will increase. It might seem that creating a much shorter loop will help, but with very short loops you'll probably find that the repeating waveform sounds more electronic than natural. That said, analogue-synth waveforms can be looped in sections as short as a single cycle, as they tend to be created from oscillators that always produce the same waveform shape. With 'real' sounds, however, very short loops rarely work.

If a difference in level is your only problem and you have the patience to do a little signal processing, you could use your sequencer's level-automation facilities to gradually 'turn up' the level of the decaying sound over the duration of the section that you wish to loop so that it's as constant as possible. You could then record the modified part as a new audio file, with all of the level changes made permanent, and then use that as the basis for your sample.

Another option (where available) is to use a looping mode that plays the looped section alternately forwards and then in reverse. Many instruments create waveforms that sound more or less the same when played backwards, so this is a viable option for disguising small changes in level or timbral in a sampled sound.

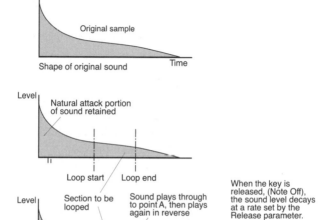

Even though the original section is
decaying in level, using forward/reverse
alternate looping ensures no level steps
occur at the loop boundaries. However,
if the loop is too short, the resulting level
modulation will be audible as the sound
alternately falls and rises in level

Figure 3.3: Forward/reverse looping

When the loop is played back, the changes will still be there but will gradually change backwards and forwards between the two sounds rather than abruptly at the loop end. Figure 3.3 shows how this forward/reverse looping works.

Modulated Sounds

Getting looping right is a matter of experience, and if the original sound has any trace of vibrato or other modulation on it, the job becomes even more difficult. In such cases, it's essential to make the loop time a multiple of the modulation rate, too, or the modulation will become irregular. In the case of a pronounced modulation of level or tremolo, it's not difficult to pick the start and end points of a loop that begins between cycles or at the peaks of cycles (it doesn't matter where you start your loop relative to the modulation, as long as the loop-end point occurs at the same place in the modulation cycle), but in the case of more subtle modulations, such as a flute that includes both amplitude and pitch modulation, you might have to try a number of options before you find one that works adequately well. As a rule, the longer you can make a loop, the more natural it will sound, but this has to be balanced against the rate at which the sound level decays or changes in timbre. This is why it's best to work with uneffected, unmodulated source material

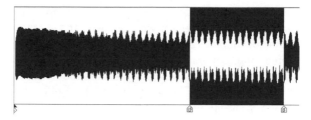

Figure 3.4: Forward/reverse looping

when looping, wherever possible. Figure 3.4 shows a modulated sound with suitable loop points set up.

Once you've tried editing your own samples, you'll realise why commercial sample CD-ROMs are so expensive – because you have to find a loop point for every sample in a multisample set! Having said that, I've found that creating and looping my own samples using a software sampler with graphical editing is far, far easier than it ever was on any typical hardware sampler.

Stereo Samples

These days, virtually all samplers support the playback of stereo samples, which take up twice as much RAM as mono samples. Not only that, but they're also more difficult to loop, as the waveforms in both channels are different and might not be exactly in phase with each

other. What constitutes a good, click-free loop point
for one channel might not work so well for the other.
Crossfade looping can rescue an otherwise impossible
stereo loop, but you have to be doubly careful when
you're checking that you have the best loop points.
With this in mind, a sample played at a high pitch can
show up an imperfect loop. If you can hear a fast,
rhythmic modulation, then your looping may be to
blame. If you have a sound that includes panning
information, it's important to find a loop-end point that
has the same stereo balance as the corresponding loop-
start point, and this is something that's much easier
to do on a software sampler with an on-screen editor
or a hardware sampler with a waveform display.
Ultimately, though, it's your ears that have to decide
whether the edit is good enough or not.

Multiple Loops

A few of the more esoteric samplers currently available
support multiple loops, which means that, instead of
having one very long loop, you can set up two or more
shorter ones. The way in which the loops are arranged
depends greatly on the sampler you're using – some
allow you to set up a different release loop to the one
that plays while you hold down a key (ie a sustain
loop), but this degree of sophistication is really beyond
the scope of this book. Most samplers have the facility

to set up just a single loop that continues to play until
the key has been released and the envelope shaper
completes the Decay part of its operation.

Trigger Modes

Not all sampler sounds benefit from being triggered in
the same way – for example, single-hit drum or cymbal
sounds should normally be allowed to play all the way
through, no matter how long a key is depressed for. To
achieve the necessary flexibility, there are two main
trigger modes: One Shot, where the sample always
plays to the end, regardless of whether the key remains
held or not, and the more conventional Retrigger mode,
whereby the sample goes into its Release phase as
soon as the key is released. One Shot mode is useful
for triggering drum loops and individual drum sounds,
whereas Retrigger mode is used for most conventional-
instrument sounds. Different manufactures may use
slightly different terminology to describe these modes
of operation, but the vast majority of samplers support
at least these two basic triggering modes.

ADSR Envelopes

Traditional analogue synthesisers create sound by
feeding a fixed waveform oscillator through a filter and
then through an envelope shaper that can control the
Attack, Decay, Sustain and Release phases of the

sound, where Attack, Decay and Release are measured in time while Sustain is a level, expressed as a percentage of the original level. Figure 3.5 shows a typical ADSR envelope.

With a looped sample, the Attack characteristics (ie the way in which the sound starts) might be the same as those of the original instrument, but the Decay portion might have been replaced by a loop which can cycle around indefinitely. For instruments that have a natural decay, such as plucked strings, this means that there must be some means of fading out the sound at the end of the note, so an ADSR-type envelope shaper is used, enabling the level of the sampled sound to be

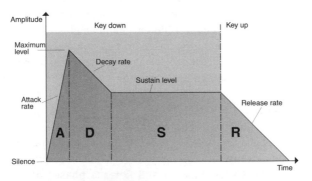

Figure 3.5: A typical ADSR envelope

changed over time, much like a synth sound. Again, some models of sampler provide more comprehensive envelope-shaping capabilities, but the basic ADSR is the most common and also the easiest to understand.

The Attack portion of the envelope is simply the time it takes for the amplitude to reach its maximum level, and so for percussive sounds the Attack time should be as short as possible. Meanwhile, slow string sounds require a longer Attack time. Then, once the sound has reached its maximum level, it starts to decay at a rate determined by the Decay setting. The sound then continues to decay until it reaches a level known as the Sustain level (another user-variable parameter), and it remains at this level for as long as the key is held down. Once the key is released, the sound resumes its decay, this time at a new rate determined by the envelope's Release setting.

Both software and hardware samplers can also include resonant-filter sections similar to those found in synthesisers. These filters may be controlled by envelopes and LFOs (Low-Frequency Oscillators), making it possible for the user to create some very analogue-synth-like sounds. Indeed, if you start off with looped samples of basic analogue-synth waveforms, it's possible to create some very authentic emulations of such synths, and because the samples are generally to a length of only a single waveform, they take up very little sample memory.

Envelope generators are most often associated with level (amplitude) control, but they also control analogue-style filter sweeps (a filter can be thought of as a remote-controlled tone control). By controlling a filter's frequency from an envelope generator, you can create a huge range of tonal sweep sounds, ranging from a slow, lazy change in timbre to a resonant twang.

It's also common to be able to invert the output of an envelope generator so that the filter sweeps from low to high instead of from high to low. However, as with the filters found in a synthesiser, sampler filters provide more than just basic tone control and invariably have an adjustable resonance facility that enables them to create strong wah-wah-like effects.

Resonant Filters

Synth filters were developed to add interest to the tonally static sounds of basic waveform oscillators. The problem is that simply mixing the basic sine, square (pulse) and triangle waveforms doesn't provide a broad enough range of timbres, and also real sounds very often change in timbre as they develop. This latter feature is something that filters can help to emulate. A picked string, for example, produces a sound that is initially rich in high-frequency harmonics, but as the sound decays, these harmonics die away faster than the fundamental frequency. When you consider the different types of sounds that can be squeezed from a simple analogue synth, imagine what the same filter and envelope facilities can do when you're working with samples!

A synth filter is in some ways like a single-band parametric equaliser with a frequency setting that can be controlled by a keyboard-triggered envelope or by other sources, such as a physical knob, key position, key velocity and so on. Whereas a parametric equaliser offers only bandpass filtering, a synth filter often offers a choice of low-pass, bandpass and high-pass filtering, all with adjustable resonance. Many samplers have a similar filter section, although the simplest will have only a resonant bandpass filter.

Like oscillators, filters may be controlled from a keyboard (in which case the higher the note you play, the higher the filter frequency), from an envelope generator or from an LFO, resulting in a filter characteristic that varies rather than remains static. Simpler synths and samplers split the use of the same envelope generator between the filter and the output level, although these days most have separate envelope generators for each function, as obviously there's more flexibility in being able to set up one envelope for the filter and a different one for the amplitude.

Types Of Filter

The filter circuits in most synthesisers operate as high-pass, bandpass or low-pass filters, based on those used in the original analogue instruments, although more complex filter types are possible. If an instrument has only one filter type, it's invariably low-pass in nature, which means that it passes only frequencies below the frequency to which it is set. The slope or sharpness of the filter is usually 12dB per octave or, in some cases, 24dB per octave, depending on the preferences of the manufacturer. The more decibels per octave, the sharper the sound of the filter. The filter slope (ie the number of dabs per octave) influences the tonal character of the instrument, which is one reason why two synths offering apparently identical facilities might sound quite different.

The addition of a Q or Resonance control greatly increases the creative potential of a filter, and increasing this value emphasises harmonics at the filter's cut-off frequency, rather like a wah-wah pedal. If the filter

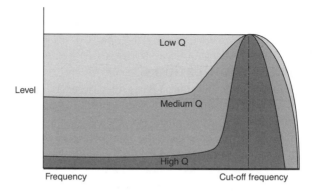

Note that some filters automatically reduce the level of the signal below the cut-off frequency as the Q is increased in order to avoid distortion. This is the system shown here

Figure 3.6: Action of a resonant low-pass filter

frequency is then varied, the familiar filter sweep sound is produced. The graph in Figure 3.6 shows the effect of varying the Resonance of a low-pass filter. By adjusting the starting frequency of the filter and then setting the rate, depth and direction of the sweep under ADSR control, a wide range of dynamically changing timbres can be created. Note that software synthesisers are more likely to include multiple filter types than hardware instruments, as their onscreen interfaces make it easier to select and control them. Very often, there will be several choices of filter slope, as well as a choice of high-, low- or bandpass operation.

Filter Applications

Not every patch includes a fierce filter sweep, but that's not to say that the filter isn't being used. For example, a mellow string pad might use the filter as a simple top-cut control to reduce the high-frequency content of a sound, or it might be linked to the velocity of the keys in order to make louder sounds brighter. In this latter mode, the filter isn't necessarily controlled from the envelope at all; increasing the Q slightly will produce a sharper, more tightly focused sound that helps to cut through a mix, while adding a little keyboard control into the filter's control input makes the filter frequency dependent on the note being played. This can be useful if you're trying to simulate an instrument that sounds brighter on the higher notes and more mellow on the lower notes.

Most classic synth-bass sounds are based on simple analogue waveforms set to a lower octave. Fashionable techno-bass sounds, meanwhile, tend to make use of fast attack times and fairly high Q settings, and if the direction of filter sweep can be inverted, this produces interesting alternatives. A fast release time on both filter and VCA (Voltage-Controlled Amplifier) envelopes helps to create a tight, well-defined bass sound, whereas longer release times might be better suited to more atmospheric music or deep bass sounds.

Classic filter-sweep sounds tend to use Q settings so high that the filter is almost (but not quite) oscillating, and either a long attack or release so as to create a dramatic sweep effect. In all cases where envelope control is being used, the manual control on the filter sets the starting state of the filter and the envelope level sets the range of the sweep. Filter sweeps can also be used rhythmically, something that's easiest to set up using a sequencer. Both hardware and software samplers can be automated by 'drawing' MIDI control information directly into the Graphical Automation page of a sequencer, and this is a useful ploy for creating filter effects that operate rhythmically.

Sample-And-Hold Filters

Filters can be controlled from a number of sources, limited only by the patching arrangements of the particular instrument you're using. One very popular effect is achieved by feeding a random, stepped waveform into the control input of the filter. If the filter is adjusted to a high Q setting, the result is a kind of wah-wah effect that jumps instantaneously from one random position to the next at a user-defined rate. In earlier analogue synthesisers, setting up this so-called 'sample and hold' effect was created by measuring or sampling the output of a random noise generator at regular intervals under the control of a low-frequency oscillator. This randomly sampled voltage would then be used to control the filter frequency. In modern synths and samplers, however, you're more likely to find the effect built in as a ready-made filter option. If you can synchronise the effect to the tempo of your song, it can be a useful rhythmic effect for dance music and associated styles.

Modulation

Today's samplers have as many modulation options as most synthesisers, some of which have been mentioned already — for example, controlling level using an envelope shaper is a form of modulation, as is using an LFO linked to the keyboard's modulation wheel to introduce vibrato. However, there are many more modulation options that can be used to make instruments sound more realistic or more interesting, such as linking release time to keyboard position, which provides a very easy way of setting up a piano-like response, where the high notes sustain for a shorter time than the low notes.

When setting up flute sounds, it's invariably better to sample these without vibrato and then add your own using LFO level modulation. If you sample a flute with vibrato, not only will it be more difficult to loop, but the vibrato will also get faster as the sample is transposed higher up the keyboard. However, a real flute's vibrato comprises both level and pitch modulation, so you need to route the LFO to control both level and pitch, then adjust the relative amounts until the result seems natural. In fact, for even greater accuracy, you could also use the LFO to modulate the filter cut-off frequency, as natural flute vibrato also includes a modulation in brightness.

Other areas to explore are linking depths of modulation or rates of attack envelope to keyboard velocity, using aftertouch to add vibrato or changing the filter settings to brighten up a sound. Tasteful use of modulation can make emulations of real instruments sound more natural and can also lend electronic sounds a more organic quality. It's also worth using a sustain pedal for changing the decay characteristics of string sounds – pedals aren't just useful for piano sounds.

Multisampling

Most 'real instrument' sounds become quite unnatural when transposed very far from their original pitch, which in some situations can be a creative advantage, but it works against you when you want a sampled instrument

basic Sampling

to sound as lifelike as possible. This problem is particularly true of pianos, and with these instruments the only way to maintain a natural sound is to take several samples at different pitches and then use each sample over only a limited part of the keyboard. Ideally, you'd take a fresh sample each semitone, but this eats up lots of memory and is a practice generally used only for the creation of very high-quality piano samples. In practice, using the same sample over a range of three or four semitones is generally accurate enough for all but the most critical instruments, and often you can get away with far fewer. As I said, pianos are the most critical, while bowed strings and wind instruments are more forgiving.

A set of samples is made up of *keygroups*, with each keygroup based around its own sample. For the most natural results, it's usually best to set up a keygroup so that each note is transposed to an equal degree in either direction of the sample's original pitch. In other words, the original sampled note should be in the middle of its keygroup. Figure 3.7 shows how a keygroup is set up.

It's also common to be able to use more than one sample in a keygroup, using keyboard velocity to decide which sample should play. On some models, you can

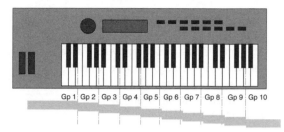

The keyboard range is divided into keygroups, where one sample is pitch-shifted to provide all of the notes within its keygroup. In this example, the keygroups are five semitones wide. The number of multisamples required depends on the characteristics of the instrument being sampled and on the degree of accuracy demanded by the user. Instruments that support velocity cross-switching or crossfading may have several samples per keygroup, each corresponding to different playing velocities. Keygroups at the upper and lower natural ranges of the instrument may be extented to cover the upper and lower limits of the keyboard, if required.

Figure 3.7: Creating a keygroup

either blend the samples according to their velocities or switch between them at a certain MIDI Velocity value. Blending can sound smoother, but in this case, because two samples are always playing at the same time you can use up to twice as much polyphony.

Sometimes you can use velocity-switching to move between quite different sounds, such as slap-/pull-bass samples, where lower velocities trigger a plucked sample and high velocities trigger a slapped or pulled sample. Other uses include wind instruments that are sampled with an overblown sound at higher velocities or instruments that sound noticeably different in some other way when played loud. In general, instruments tend to sound brighter when played louder, and this can be faked to some extent by linking the sampler's filter to MIDI Velocity.

Keygroups And Drums

Drum-set samples rely very heavily on keygroups because they tend to comprise many different samples, often with a single sample – kick drum or snare, for example – assigned to a single key. Each of these sounds is assigned its own keygroup, and it's normal to disable the keyboard's Pitch Tracking so that the samples play back at their original pitches. A useful technique is to set up two occurrences of each drum sample so that you can play two different keys with two fingers, which makes playing rolls and fills easier. Where you position them is up to you, but it's best to find a system and then stick to it so you don't find that every drum kit you call up has all of the drums in different places. As a rule, a polyphony of one or two notes works best for drum sounds, with the trigger mode set for One Shot.

Occasionally, you might wish to include some tunable elements in a drum kit, such as an octave of tuned toms or marimbas. Again, this can be achieved using keygroups, but this time with the Pitch Tracking active. With hi-hats, you might wish to assign these to separate groups, with one-note polyphony, so that it's impossible to get the open and closed hi-hats sounding together. (This concept is discussed more fully later in the chapter, in 'Groups And Outputs'.) You'll probably also find that you can use different pan positions for individual keygroups – again, a useful feature for drum-kit samples.

Time And Pitch Manipulation

Pitch Change and Time Stretch are commands supported by many hardware samplers, allowing the user to change the pitch of a sound independently of its length and vice versa. These facilities are invaluable for massaging audio-sample loops, but it's important to know that the processes involved often introduce audible side-effects, and that the further the audio is processed from its original pitch or tempo, the more audible these side-effects tend to be. The technology used here is similar to that used in pitch-shifting effects units, and although this isn't the appropriate place for a full description of how these work, it's useful to know that the process involves slicing the audio into very small sections and then rejoining them. It's the joins between these slices that cause the side-effects. Non-real-time processes often sound better than time/pitch

basic Sampling

manipulation that takes place in real time, and this is the way in which most hardware samplers work.

The most useful process here is time-stretching, which can be used to make a section of music longer or shorter without changing its pitch. This is clearly useful when you want to make two loops of slightly different tempos work together in sync – you simply work out the percentage of change needed to make the errant loop fit and then process it. Typically, it's possible to change loop lengths by up to ten per cent without incurring too many side-effects, although if you attempt anything beyond this, the quality can start to get gritty. As with just about any side-effect, from aliasing to distortion, the dance-music fraternity has used the by-products of extreme time-stretching as a creative process, and it's not unknown for someone to take a perfectly clean loop, apply a time stretch of 100 per cent and then repeat the process in the opposite direction to get back to the original tempo, but this time with all of the crunchy processing side-effects present.

Changing pitch independent of tempo can be useful for subtly changing the character of a voice or for making even more drastic changes. The result is very similar to what you might expect from a hardware pitch-shifting unit, although the quality might be better where non-real-time processing is used to process the audio sample.

With software samplers that run as plug-ins, it's usually necessary to use the audio-processing capabilities of the host sequencer to handle any time-manipulation prior to creating samples.

Programs

A playable sampler instrument comprises one or more samples assigned to keygroups, which may or may not be looped, plus all of the necessary filter and envelope settings. It's pretty obvious that you don't want to load individual samples every time you want to use a multisampled instrument, so the necessary samples are arranged into programs, along with their looping, filter, envelope and modulation data. When a program is loaded into memory, the complete multisampled instrument is ready to play.

It's also quite possible to make many different programs out of one set of samples or by combining different sets of samples – for example, a multisampled string sound could be used in a slow-attack program, with a fast-attack program and perhaps variations with different filter settings used for warm strings or bright strings. Alternatively, you could layer a synth-string multisample with an orchestral-string multisample and save it as a new hybrid. Software samplers make layering in this way extremely easy, normally allowing you to use the computer's Copy and Paste functions to transfer program information from one program to another. While samples are rather large pieces of data, the programs themselves are very small, as they contain information concerning only which samples to use, where to loop them and which filter, envelope and modulation settings are needed. This means that you can create lots of programs from the same samples without using up significant amounts of RAM.

Groups And Outputs

Typical serious samplers include a system of grouping samples so that, instead of all parameters acting globally, different settings can be applied to different groups. Furthermore, if the sampler supports multiple outputs, it's usually possible to route these groups to different physical outputs. (This is most useful when setting up drum programs as you'll often want to keep the kick and snare drums separate from the rest of the kit so that you can process them differently.) You can also have different polyphony settings within groups, which is particularly important for when you only ever want one hi-hat sample to play at once, for instance;

by assigning all of your hi-hat samples to the same group and them setting the polyphony value to 1, closed hi-hats will always cut off open hi-hats, just as they do in real life.

Groups are also useful if you want to create a keyboard split with, say, a monophonic synth bass on the left and a polyphonic piano on the right. All you have to do is assign your synth-bass parts to a group with a polyphony of 1 and the piano sounds to a group with whichever level of polyphony you require. As hardware samplers have limited polyphony, and this must be shared between all of the parts of a multisample, it makes sense to set the lowest polyphony levels that you can get away with.

Other features that you might find in groups include the ability to delay the start of the level-envelope generator relative to other groups. This makes setting up a layered patch where one sound comes in after another a straightforward task. If your sampler has internal digital effects, you'll probably find that you can use different settings or levels of effect on different groups. Each sampler offers slightly different features in this area, so take the time to read the manual that came with yours to see what tricks you can pull off by using its grouping capabilities.

Multitimbrality

A sampler program (sometimes called an *instrument*, depending on the manufacturer) is a playable set of samples including all of the necessary settings. However, if you want to use your sampler multitimbrally, you'll need to set up several programs and assign each to a different MIDI channel. With a software sampler, this is extremely easy, as all you have to do is open up a separate sampler for each of the parts and assign each its own sequencer track.

Different hardware samplers do the job in different ways, but most use a variation of Akai's Multi, a special type of program that holds the information about which 'single' programs are to be used on which MIDI channel. When you load up a Multi, all of the necessary samples for all of the parts are loaded, along with their program data and MIDI-channel assignments. Note, however, that, because of the memory limitations on some earlier hardware samplers, these might not have enough RAM to support full multitimbral operation, depending on the sizes of the samples you wish to load.

Spinning In

In the days of recording before samplers, a technique known as *spinning in* was used regularly when parts needed to be added to a multitrack recording. For example, if a singer managed only one really good chorus take, this would be copied to an open-reel, two-track tape machine and then copied back to the other chorus positions on the master multitrack tape. Getting the playback to start at exactly the right time involved marking the tape with wax pencil and other tricks of this kind, but as it was the only technique in town that could achieve the desired result, engineers became very proficient at it. Once good-sounding 16-bit samplers with sufficient memory became available at affordable prices, samplers replaced the open-reel recorders when it came to spinning in copied parts, either by manual triggering or under MIDI control.

Hard-disk audio workstations are able to do this kind of 'copy and move' edit very simply, but when working with tape-based systems, samplers are still useful in this respect. The technique can be used at a number of levels, from replacing specific instrumental or vocal sections to assembling entire songs. As a rule, the sampler would be triggered from a sequencer synchronised to tape in order to keep the timing precise. With analogue tape, where speed is liable to drift slightly, the sampled sections should be kept as short as is practicable in order to prevent them from slipping out of time.

Summary

The process of sampling isn't difficult, but it can be time-consuming, especially where multisampling and looping is required. If you plan to make a lot of your own multisamples, I'd suggest that you use either a software sampler or a hardware sampler that has computer-editing software available for it, as using one of these is much easier than peering into a tiny LCD window. MIDI may be used to transfer samples between a sampler and a computer, but it is mind-numbingly slow; a system that can transfer samples over SCSI is much more satisfactory.

With a sampler, you can load library samples that produce all of the sounds available on conventional synths, but often of a much better quality because of the greater sampling time available. Typical synths cram every single sound into 16Mb or 32Mb of memory, where a typical sample will use that much just for one orchestral sound, and a really good piano program can be anything up to a couple of gigabytes!

The sampler can also replace your drum machine, and again just about every conceivable drum sound is available in sample libraries. In addition to complete drum kits, where different drum sounds are mapped to all keys, there are library files of numerous drum and percussion loops available, played by top professionals, as well as instrumental riffs and phrases, vocal phrases and even orchestral construction kits, which allow you to build music from a set of interlocking phrases. Although these sample CDs and CD-ROMs can be expensive, they relieve you of an enormous amount of work. CD-ROMs cost more than audio sample CDs, but these do all the looping and keygrouping work for you; audio CDs, on the other hand, are just recordings of individual audio samples, which you still have to loop and organise into keygroups, so I strongly recommend that anyone who has an older sampler without a CD-ROM drive should get one as soon as possible. Most library CD-ROMs are supplied in a format readable by Akai samplers, but current Roland, Akai and E-mu models will usually read each other's formats without too much problem.

4 SOFTWARE SAMPLERS

While samplers started out in hardware form, they all employ digital technology that's very similar to that used inside a computer, so it was inevitable that someone would develop a computer-based sampler that would need no hardware, other than some type of audio interface over which to record and play sound. Early soft samplers required additional DSP (Digital Signal Processing) cards to handle the processing load, but these days host-based software instruments are common, where 'host-based' means that all of the processing work is carried out by the computer running the software.

Most users want to use sampling in tandem with a MIDI sequencer, so the stand-alone software sampler has now been largely replaced by the so-called *plug-in*. A plug-in is essentially a piece of software that works from within a host software application rather than runs separately as an application in its own right.

Stand-alone programs may still be able to integrate with

a host sequencer to some extent by utilising technologies such as ReWire, but both the plug-in and the sequencer must be ReWire-compatible for this to work. A stand-alone software sampler running on a separate computer fitted with a MIDI interface and soundcard may also be connected to a sequencer via MIDI in the same way as a hardware instrument.

ReWire

OK, so what's ReWire, exactly? Well, ReWire is a joint development between Steinberg and Propellerhead that allows audio to be routed between different programs in real time. It is available for both Mac and PC platforms and can be thought of as a multichannel software audio cable – rather like a piece of multicore, in fact. This virtual multicore can accommodate up to 64 channels of audio synchronised to single-sample accuracy at any one time (possibly more channels in later revisions), and at any standard bit resolution and sample rate. Basic transport commands such as Play and Stop can also be sent via ReWire, which is important for those software instruments that include some kind of sequencing function, such as Propellerhead's ReBirth virtual analogue drum/bass synth. Using ReWire, it's possible to patch the output from a virtual instrument directly into the mixer section of the host sequencer, where it can be mixed and processed like any other audio track or source.

Plug-ins

The first company to take the plug-in concept seriously was Digidesign, and when they had the foresight to open up plug-in manufacture to third-party developers, they provided the basis of a very powerful audio-recording and -mixing system.

Today, Digidesign produce plug-ins in their AudioSuite range, which can be used with Pro Tools 4 and upwards, plus the TDM (Time Division Multiplexing) real-time range, which runs exclusively on Pro Tools hardware. Some other software manufacturers also support AudioSuite plug-ins (both non-real-time models and the real-time RTAS variant), as well as their own real-time plug-in formats, and sequencers that can support Pro Tools hardware can generally access TDM plug-ins.

On the PC side, Microsoft created Direct X as a part of the multimedia aspect of Windows, and this program handles both DirectSound soundcard drivers and DirectShow plug-ins (often still referred to as Direct X). Most Windows music software supports this plug-in architecture, with a lot also supporting VST (Virtual Studio Technology) effects and instruments, discussed shortly.

Somebody once said that it was because standards are so good that there are so many of them, and sadly not everyone wants to support the same plug-in format, especially if – as in the case of Steinberg's VST – it was developed by a potential rival. For example, MOTU (Mark Of The Unicorn) developed their own format, MAS, for use with the Mac version of their Digital Performer sequencing software, and Cakewalk Sonar also has its own format.

However, the most popular standard at this time is undoubtedly VST, which is supported on both Mac and PC platforms. The latest incarnation, VST II, can both generate and be controlled by MIDI, which opens up the field for plug-in automation, as well as making it possible for manufacturers to produce VST instruments such as virtual synths and samplers.

VST Plug-ins

The VST plug-in format was created by Steinberg to enable software-generated effects to be added to audio tracks within the mixing environment of a MIDI-plus-audio sequencer. By making the VST protocol openly available to anyone who wanted to use it, Steinberg brought us as close to a plug-in standard as we're likely to get (even though, as I pointed out earlier, not all music software provides VST support). These days, various third-party companies produce VST-compatible plug-ins for both PC and Macintosh computers.

basic Sampling

The two major players (at least in Europe) are Steinberg's Cubase VST and Emagic's Logic Audio. Both of these programs can run VST plug-ins, as can many stereo editing packages, and because VST development information is freely available to anyone who wants to use it, a number of shareware and freeware plug-ins have been created by enthusiasts to augment the already impressive list of commercial offerings.

VST plug-ins are placed within a VST folder on the hard drive of the computer, where they can be accessed by any audio program that is VST-compatible; in other words, you can use the same VST plug-ins in your MIDI-plus-audio sequencer as in your stereo editor. The first time you try to run a VST plug-in from a newly installed piece of audio software, you may be asked to locate the VST folder. Programs often come bundled with their own sets of VST plug-ins, so if you find you've ended up with more than one VST folder, it's probably best to move all of your VST plug-ins to a single folder and then direct the software to use this folder the next time it asks where your VST plug-ins are located.

The exact means of accessing virtual-instrument plug-ins varies from sequencer to sequencer, but they generally end up being routed through audio channels within the virtual mixing section of the host sequencer program.

When they were first introduced, VST plug-ins could be set up via onscreen controls, and user settings could be saved and called up later, but there was no way of adjusting the plug-in parameters automatically while playing a piece of music on the sequencer. Clearly, the concept of automation has a lot of creative potential, so Steinberg came up with the VST II standard, which allows plug-in parameters to be controlled via MIDI information, in much the same way as hardware effects boxes can be controlled via MIDI.

Virtual synths and samplers can have graphically sophisticated control interfaces, often with more knobs and sliders than their hardware counterparts. In the case of VST and other, similar plug-in formats, real-time changes to these controls can be recorded into the host MIDI sequencer, providing a very easy way of automating control changes. Dance-music composers use automation a great deal for adding filter sweeps or changes in cut-off frequency.

Note that existing VST plug-ins cannot be used with Mac OS X, so a revised VST format will need to be developed. Some manufacturers may support 'Apple Audio Units' directly rather than revamp VST, as it is a part of the OS that is able to achieve the same results as VST but without any of the potential complications that may result from the technology and development of VST being controlled by a single manufacturer.

Sample Formats

The majority of software samplers can read at least some of the CD-ROM library formats produced for commercial hardware samplers, the most common of which are the Akai S1000 and S3000 formats followed by E-mu and Roland, although support for alternative formats such as SoundFont II and GigaSampler are also included in some models. Whereas hardware samplers have their own RAM, software samplers tend to utilise the host computer's RAM, so it makes sense to install as much as possible if you intend to make serious use of a software sampler.

Even RAM has a limit, though, which is why GigaSampler introduced the idea of streaming samples directly from a computer's hard drive, thus saving on RAM and allowing longer samples to be used. The basics of the GigaSampler concept are that only the starts of samples are held in RAM. When a note is played, there is a seamless transition of data being streamed from the hard drive, allowing samples of almost unlimited length to be played back. Other software samplers have since implemented their own methods of streaming from disk, and some of these support GigaSampler libraries. Where streaming technology really comes into its own, however, is in the playback of things like high-quality grand piano multisamples, where each individual note is sampled for its full duration at a variety of playing intensities and pedal settings. This can easily result in a set of samples over a gigabyte in size, which is clearly asking a lot of a purely RAM-based sampler! Using hard-disk streaming in this way also reduces the loading time for long samples (loading a 1Gb piano into RAM would be next to interminable) and may also improve the polyphony available for a given CPU load.

Virtual Pros And Cons

While virtual instruments are clearly now a very important part of music making today, they still have limitations, the most obvious being their drain on processing resources. As a rule, the more notes you play at once, the more computing power is required. Furthermore, adding effects or filters will also increase the processing load. However, a well-designed sampler is often quite efficient, compared to some software synths, and a modern computer should be able to handle a reasonable number of virtual instruments and virtual effects at once.

Software samplers have several advantages over their hardware counterparts, not least being that most have a clearer onscreen graphical interface. Furthermore, instead of employing arcane multitimbral modes, you can simply open a separate sampler in each track on which you need sample playback (although some software instruments and samplers still have multitimbral capabilities, if required). Also, having a plug-in software sampler that can run within a host sequencer that supports a plug-in effects format (such as VST) means that the sampler's output can be further processed with standard plug-in effect, such as delay, chorus or reverb. You can even use separate plug-ins for each track, up to the limit of your computer's processing capacity.

The other great benefit is that the computer's own RAM – or even hard-disk streaming – is used for sample playback, so the available sample memory is usually much greater than you'd get from a conventional hardware instrument. However, you should note that some older hardware samplers use specially designed memory cards which are very expensive in comparison with computer memory. Furthermore, many of these older models are limited to a maximum of 32Mb of memory, so even fully expanded they have a very limited capacity, especially if used multitimbrally. Because of these limitations, older models tend to make a poor second-hand buy, especially if they don't come with a fully expanded memory, so beware of apparent bargains.

There are numerous soft samplers available, but there might be some advantages in buying one that's designed specifically to run within the sequencer program you normally use. Not least of these is the host software's ability to access the sampler directly, so that its editing capabilities can be used for sample editing, but you might also find that a sampler written for a particular sequencer package runs more efficiently than a general-purpose plug-in sampler, as there might be a saving on CPU resources.

To take an example, Emagic's EXS24 sampler is designed specifically for users of that company's Logic Audio program and handles file imports from a number of commercial formats (as well as having its own EXS24-format library disks) by converting samples to its own format and then storing them on the computer's hard drive. As drive space is now very cheap, this is a very practical way of working, and one advantage of this technique that you'll notice right away is that samples stored on a hard drive load up in seconds, whereas on a hardware sampler using a CD-ROM library they can take a couple of minutes. Samples are selected for loading via a pull-down menu, rather like synth patches.

Whereas conventional audio tracks rely on disk access, samplers work directly from RAM, so there's no drain on disk-access capacity, other than when you're actually loading or saving samples. Furthermore, because the sampler doesn't have to create sounds in real time, the processing load tends to be smaller than in the case of a software synthesiser (although filters and onboard effects add to the processor load when used).

Some software samplers, such as GigaSampler, include a mixer, allowing you to combine different multitimbral parts, and some may also come with software effects, such as reverb and delay, that can be deployed within the mixer.

Sample Libraries

Ready-made libraries of instrument samples, sound effects and drum loops are available for most of the common makes of sampler, generally on CD-ROM, with the Akai sampler format being most prevalent. These disks might seem expensive, but they generally include a licence (for the original purchaser only) allowing you to use the material within a commercial musical composition without having to pay any additional royalties. Terms and conditions vary between suppliers, though, so it pays to check the small print.

Software Drivers

Hardware is linked to your sequencing software by an invisible piece of computer code known as a *driver*, so in order for your system to work, a driver must exist that is compatible with both the host sequencer software and the hardware interface. If your host software and your audio hardware both support ASIO or ASIO II, it's reasonably safe to assume that the two will work together, provided that the driver works properly. I make this latter point because the various hardware manufacturers' internet sites frequently feature updated driver software that either improves the performance of or fixes bugs in their drivers.

ASIO

ASIO stands for Audio Stream Input/Output and is a technology first designed as a part of the Cubase VST software. Its latest incarnation, ASIO II, is another Steinberg innovation, establishing a standard protocol for audio drivers that bypass the slower parts of the host computer's operating system and that can be shared across platforms and between other manufacturers who support the protocol. ASIO and ASIO II also support soundcards with multiple inputs and outputs, so the technology isn't limited to stereo audio handling. If a sequencer is ASIO II compatible and the audio hardware (soundcard or audio interface) comes with ASIO II drivers,

basic Sampling

also find buffer-size settings in your driver software's control panel, so experiment to find the shortest buffer size that you can use without compromising the system's performance reliability. The latency figure may be expressed in milliseconds or in samples, where settings of 512 samples or below usually feel OK for real-time playing at 44.1kHz sample rates or higher.

Of course, you might have a system that doesn't support ASIO II drivers, or your software might but your hardware might not. Alternatively, you might just be one of those people who are very sensitive to timing and for whom even minimal latency is too much. What then?

The only solution to high latency values when working with virtual instruments of any kind, including samplers, is to use a hardware instrument as a substitute when recording (an external MIDI synth or a soundcard's onboard synth), then switch back to the virtual instrument for playback. Playback is no problem – the host software should automatically compensate for latency, as playback need not be a real-time operation; a 500ms delay when you press the Play button isn't nearly as serious as a 500ms delay when you press a key and expect to hear a note. Having said that, any properly conceived Mac or PC system should be able to operate with under 10ms of latency, which most

Software Samplers

players find completely undetectable. Problems usually arise when general-purpose computer-game soundcards are used rather than audio interfaces designed specifically for serious audio work. As a rule, as long as your computer is reasonably up to date, latency problems can usually be traced either to inappropriate combinations of audio hardware and drivers or to incorrect settings for driver buffer sizes.

5 RECORDING YOUR OWN SAMPLES

Creating your own samples and programs can be relatively easy, or it can be quite time consuming, but none of the individual stages are actually that difficult. You just need to take into account certain factors when recording and editing your samples.

The first stage in sampling is to record your audio into the sampler, although in the case of multisampled instruments, you might find it more straightforward to first record the individual notes using a DAT or MiniDisc machine; this way, you can take more sampled notes than you think you'll ultimately need and then select which samples to transfer into your sampler – via its digital input, if it has one. You should approach the recording as you would any other studio recording and experiment with microphone positions to get the best possible sound. The fastest way of doing this is to monitor the output of the recorder or sampler using fully enclosed headphones (the type that cut out most of the sound from the outside world) and then move the mic around while listening to the way the sound changes. When you've found the best spot, place the mic on a stand and work with that position for all of your samples.

When sounds are recorded into a sampler, sounds with distinct attacks can usually be entrusted to the Automatic Record trigger mode, if your sampler has one, but slow-attack sounds may work better if you start recording manually and then trim the start times of the samples afterwards. Software samplers tend not to have automatic triggering modes, but because the samples can be viewed in a Waveform Edit window, trimming start points and setting loop points is quick and easy.

Mono Or Stereo?

Before you can record your own samples, you're going to need a mic, and if your sampler doesn't have a mic input (or if you're using a software sampler), you'll need to use a mixer or mic pre-amp. Any decent dynamic vocal mic will suffice for most basic percussion and electric guitar/bass sampling jobs, but a capacitor or back-electret mic will give better results if you're sampling more delicate acoustic-instrument sounds or vocals.

Most of the samples you create yourself will probably work just as well in mono as in stereo, as the addition of stereo reverb and panning will provide the illusion of stereo – and remember that working in mono conserves RAM and makes the job of looping rather easier. As a rule, only physically large instruments, such as pianos or drums, benefit from stereo miking, and to be honest, in most cases you're better off buying this kind of sound on a CD-ROM library than trying to sample it yourself. However, if you do come across something that would benefit from being sampled in stereo, simply use one of the traditional stereo-miking techniques, such as coincident cardioid mics (ie two cardioid mics angled at around 90° with their capsules as close together as possible) or spaced omni or cardioid mics. Crossfade looping is invariably needed when looping stereo samples, but most of the instruments I can imagine needing to be recorded in stereo could be sampled without looping – apart from the accordion, perhaps.

The subject of miking up different instruments is discussed in more depth in *Home Recording Made Easy* and *Recording & Production Techniques*, both of which are available from Sanctuary Publishing (see back page for ordering details). However, it's enough here to say that I have a very general rule for establishing a suitable mic distance, based on using the width of the sound-producing part of the instrument as the mic distance. For example, the body of an acoustic guitar is perhaps

16" long, so setting up the mic at 16" from the guitar will produce a usable sound. Once you've got the distance worked out, you can use enclosed headphones to locate the best position. Vocals should normally be close-miked using a capacitor mic with a pop shield between the mic and the singer.

Recording Levels

When it comes to getting sounds into your sampler, you must keep in mind that sampling is a digital recording process, so you need to sample at the highest possible safe level if you want the best signal-to-noise ratio and lowest distortion. As you're probably already aware, digital recorders won't tolerate clipping, so use the metering on your sampler very carefully to make sure that the peak signal level is as high as possible without actually hitting oVU.

In the case of multisamples, you'll probably find that most acoustic instruments register more loudness on their low notes than on their high notes. In this case, get the right recording level for the low notes and then use the same settings for the higher notes. Although the recorded level might appear a little on the low side, this technique will produce a natural level balance across the keyboard and should save you the trouble of adjusting the levels of your samples after recording.

Creating Keygroups

When recording several different rhythm loops or audio phrases that are at the same tempo – from an audio CD or audio CD sample library, for example – handling them will be easier if you create separate one-note-wide keygroups for each of them so that each can be triggered from its own key on the keyboard. The benefit of working in this way is that you can then play in an arrangement in real time by triggering the samples in the order you want them, or you can trigger two different samples at the same time to create a layer – for example, playing a drum loop and a percussion loop simultaneously. One Shot trigger mode is usually best for drum loops, although if you need to cut off a loop halfway through, it's best to use Gate trigger mode so that the note plays only for as long as the key is held down.

How Many Samples?

When sampling acoustic instruments, you have to decide how many samples you'll need in order to make the instrument sound realistic, and one easy way of doing this is to take one sample somewhere in the middle of the instrument's range, place it into a keygroup covering the whole range of the keyboard and then see how far it can be played from its original pitch before it starts to sound unnatural. Listen also for tonal changes, because most sounds get brighter

160

as they are shifted up in pitch and darker as they are shifted down. If these changes are too great, they'll show up at keygroup boundaries – the highest note in one keygroup will sound bright while the first note in the next keygroup up will sound comparatively dull.

Another decision you need to make is whether or not each sample sounds acceptable when played back at different loudnesses, under keyboard velocity control, or whether the loud and soft sounds are so different that you should create separate loud and soft samples and then use MIDI Velocity data to switch between them while playing. Only once you've made these decisions can you start to record the samples themselves, and with traditional (ie acoustic) instruments it's important that these are played at a consistent level, and that no vibrato or other modulation is applied – in most cases. There are exceptions to this last rule – for instance, if you need to capture a note that sounds more 'performed'. Some flutes sound much better with natural vibrato than they do with artificial vibrato added to them. However, using such samples to play a melody is often unsatisfactory, as the vibrato will always come in at the same time and at the same depth for every note, and the rate will change with pitch, unless you have lots of different samples. A real player, on the other hand, will change his or her vibrato to suit the melody and phrasing. As a rule, samples with vibrato or other performance flourishes work best when used sparsely or when mixed with straight samples. One way of achieving this is to create a multisample with velocity-switched layers so that, if a note is played above a certain threshold of velocity, the vibrato sample plays, while if it's played softer, the straight sample plays. Another trick when you're working with instruments that have a limited range is to create a two-octave section of keyboard for your vibrato samples and another two-octave section for your straight samples. You can then jump between the two.

Fine Tuning

Unfortunately, the work isn't over once you've placed all your samples into keygroups. With acoustic instruments, you should check the accuracy of their tuning (against an electronic tuner or electronic keyboard, if possible) and use the Coarse and Fine tuning controls on your sampler to correct any that are out of tune. If the sampled instrument produces sounds that decay, such as a plucked string instrument, then you may be able to use your samples exactly as they are, without having to loop them. In the early days of sampling, even this kind of sound was usually looped to save on sample memory, but unless you're using an older model with restricted memory capacity, you'll save yourself a lot of trouble, and produce better sounds, if you use full-length, unlooped samples.

The type of instrument sound that needs looping is generally also the easiest to loop, because instruments that can play long, sustaining notes can usually do so at a reasonably constant level and timbre, and the more constant the level and timbre, the easier it is to find a good loop point. Some examples of these instruments are flutes, brass, woodwind, bowed strings and organs, but once again it's usually best to omit vibrato or any other modulation from the original performance when sampling them. Organs can be sampled with or without the rotary speaker running, but if you choose to sample with it in action, you'll have to use a lot of samples to prevent the different rate of modulation at different pitches (within each keygroup) from being too obvious. You'll also need to sample 'fast', 'slow' and 'off' rotary-speaker versions and then have some way of triggering these via either velocity or modulation wheel, if possible.

Of course, sampling rotary speakers at their two speed settings misses out the acceleration effect between slow and fast that is an essential part of the musical characteristics of such systems, so my advice would be that, unless you have a very specific organ sound that you need to sample, you should use either library samples instead (which still don't have the acceleration effect) or, better still, a virtual instrument, such as Native Instruments' B4. This is a physically modelled virtual instrument that does a superb job of reproducing drawbar organ sounds, complete with overdrive, variable-drawbar harmonic control and authentic-sounding rotary-speaker simulation, with variable acceleration. One of the skills of sampling is knowing when an alternative technology will do the job better! Having said that, if you need a traditional pipe organ, there are some superb sample-library sounds available.

Sample Storage

For samplers using an integral floppy drive for sample storage, each 1.44Mb disk will hold around 15 seconds' worth of mono samples, which isn't a lot of use if you have a 32Mb memory – and 32Mb is tiny in comparison with modern hardware and software samplers. Personally, I used an Iomega Zip drive on my old Akai S2000, although a higher capacity external hard drive (often SCSI) is arguably more convenient, as with these you don't have to swap disks. However, the downside here is that you risk losing more if a hard disk becomes corrupted, so it's a good idea to use a CD-R burning program that can mount foreign disk formats to back up important samples. You might also need to install a SCSI card in your computer to allow you to connect the sampler's drive, but these are relatively inexpensive.

These days, like most studio users, I use a software sampler. While hardware samplers are essential for live performance and for use in hardware-based studios, they have been largely replaced by software samplers in those studios that rely on computer sequencing. Here the samples are stored on one of the computer's hard drives, which means that they're easier to back up with a CD-R burning program.

Drum Loops

Drum loops are most often found on sample-library CDs or CD-ROMs, although some users also lift sections from commercial audio CDs or even radio programmes. This is fine, but if you want to use a commercial sample, however small, in a record destined for release, you'll have to obtain (and pay for) copyright clearance, or you could find yourself on the wrong side of an expensive legal battle. If you're using a CD-ROM or an audio-sample CD, a licence to use that sample is included in the purchase price, but terms and conditions may still be attached and, as a rule, the licence relates only to use by the original purchaser. If you sell or lend the samples to anyone else, they have no licence to use them, and in many cases you can't even allow a musician visiting your studio to use the samples.

As I mentioned back in the Introduction, you could record a drum part into a sampler, set up a keygroup and then create a loop within the sampler that causes the drum loop to play continuously as long as the key is held down. If you're working in this way, however, the chances are that the length of the drum loop won't be exactly the same as the length of one bar in your sequencer, so over time the drum loop will drift out of sync with your sequencer. If the sequencer is synchronised to an analogue tape machine, the problem of drift tends to be much more noticeable, as the speed stability of analogue machines is not nearly as good as that of digital devices.

A more reliable option is to set the drum part up as a one-shot sample and then trigger it once every bar (or whatever the length of the drum sample) from your sequencer. This will ensure the timing doesn't drift because, at the start of each bar, sync will be established afresh. This technique is also valuable when dealing with repeating guitar riffs, and long vocal sections may also be broken down into shorter phrases and stored as separate samples if there are sync problems. Figure 5.1a illustrates the difference between

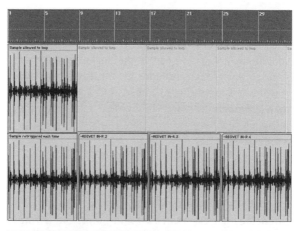

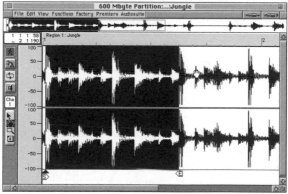

Figure 5.1a (above): Looping a drum pattern
Figure 5.1b (below): Selecting a drum loop

looping and retriggering, with the upper waveform showing a drum loop that has been set to loop continuously. You can see that the timing errors become greater with each repeat. In contrast, the lower waveform is retriggered afresh for each measure so that, although its length is slightly shorter than ideal (exaggerated here for the sake of clarity), the errors aren't cumulative.

Meanwhile, Figure 5.1b shows a drum loop being selected from a longer recorded sample. Continuous looping is a useful tool for auditioning a loop in order to ensure that the start and end points are accurate enough. Once the loop has been created, however, retriggering is the only way of ensuring that no timing errors creep in.

Creative Sampling

While few people would tackle a job like sampling a grand piano, creating your own samples can still be a rewarding experience, and that doesn't just mean finding drum loops on records or sampling sounds from your friends' keyboards. Most of the conventional sounds you're likely to need in music composition are already available in libraries, so it's usually a good idea to set out to create unusual samples that can't be found elsewhere.

In the early days of sampling, everyone tried blowing over beer bottles and sampling the outcome, and it didn't matter that the character of the sound changed wildly as you moved up the keyboard – this was being creative! Today, however, people have tired of such novelties, so it's important to strive to find something a little more imaginative.

With rhythm playing a more important part than ever in contemporary pop music, the sampler provides the perfect tool for capturing unusual sounds that can then be used in a rhythmic context. Percussive sounds don't usually need multisampling, fine tuning or looping, and so, aside from a little trimming here and there, they're often ready to be dropped into keygroups and used. You don't even need any real instruments to create some really powerful drum sounds, as you can often process everyday sounds or employ common household objects. Most of the time, all you need to do is adjust the pitch, maybe sharpen up the attack by truncating the start of the sample and adjust the envelope shape and you're there. To get you started, I've included a few examples of things that can be used to create great percussion sounds. If you have a DAT machine or MiniDisc recorder, you have the facility to record a series of samples first and then decide which ones are worth keeping before you transfer them into your sampler.

Percussion Sound Sources

Slamming a metal garage door produces a huge, powerful sound that will reverberate inside the garage (the emptier the garage, the better this will sound), so you'll get a different result depending on whether you're miking it from inside or outside. You'll probably want to trim the sound so that you use only the bang of the door slamming – you probably won't want the squeaks that come first – and if the decay time is too long, you can reduce it by using the sampler's envelope controls. Try the sound at different pitches for industrial-sounding kick- or snare-drum substitutes.

Meanwhile, a slammed wooden interior door can be retuned to create a good kick sound. Leaving a window or other door open may help in this as it prevents air pressure in the room from cushioning the slam. Also, bouncing a plastic football or basketball on a hard surface produces a very warm, resonant sound that can be tuned to sound like a deep kick drum suitable for dance music. If you want a more percussive kick sound, throwing a large ball of soggy paper against a garage door, plastic suitcase or tea chest can be surprisingly effective.

Tap any speaker cone (gently!) and you'll hear a noise, but on larger speakers, such as those used in studio monitors or instrument amplifiers, the chances are that the noise will be a deep thud, not unlike a kick drum. Mic up the speaker at close range, drop the pitch of the sample further, if need be, and you have yet another kick drum. If you don't have access to a large speaker, plastic lampshades produce a similar sound, as do taut umbrellas.

For impromptu tom sounds, you can't beat using suitcases made of plastic or, even better, one of the really old cardboard types. Try hitting one with a range of objects, including a rolled-up newspaper and a wooden mallet. Keep the mic fairly close and monitor your recording levels to make sure you don't run into clipping. A wooden tea chest also works well and may produce a longer decay time.

Snapping a wooden stick in half provides a satisfying substitute for a techno snare sound, especially if you add a bright reverb, while more unusual sounds can be made by hitting aluminium baking foil, metal radiators, trash cans or other resonant metal objects. The kitchen is always a great place to start looking for samples, and an inverted biscuit tin invariably makes a good-sounding hand drum, after which you can move to the kids' toy box or the workshop. Saw blades – now there's a wealth of sampling possibilities!

basic Sampling

Banging together a couple of lengths of well-dried 2' x 2' wood should produce a nice resonant thunk, which can then be shifted up to give you claves or down to create marimbas or log drums. Try playing the resulting sound over a couple of octaves – if the wood rings well enough, you'll probably get enough of a pitched sound to be able to create a tuned percussion set.

While vacuum cleaners are not strictly percussive, they and other motor-powered devices can be sampled and then the pitches of the samples dropped until they sound like huge, rumbling machines. If you then gate the sample and drop the pitch further, you can trigger short bursts with fast attack and fast release to produce a techno/rave feel.

Old demo tapes are also a good source for sampling. For example, if you take the kick drum from a drum fill, it may have a hi-hat playing at the same time, which produces a very well-defined kick sound with a metallic edge and lots of depth.

To create bell sounds, spanners are a must – just hang them from cotton or fishing line and tap them with a metal spoon or another spanner. Drop the pitch and you can produce some very atmospheric, Eastern-sounding bells.

Finally, don't forget to use your collection of regular instruments in a different way. Predictably enough, tapping on the body of an acoustic guitar and then dropping the pitch produces a good drum sound, but I've also had some success with tapping the strings on an electric guitar while damping them. In fact, one of my own tracks has a percussion section created entirely from a tapped electric guitar which was sampled, dropped in pitch by an octave and then reversed.

Any or all of the above sounds can be processed using regular studio effects or plug-ins before being sampled, and various degrees of distortion (from a guitar pedal) can add interest and weight to the results.

Creating Chromatic Samples

When you listen to commercial sample libraries, you'll probably come across some amazing textures and pads that go way beyond what a conventional synth can produce. Creating sounds like this requires a huge amount of skill and patience, but that doesn't mean you shouldn't try to come up with some sounds of your own, and this task is a lot faster and easier with a software sampler than it is with most hardware samplers; you don't need much equipment, only patience.

Textural samples are sometimes designed to be used

as pads while others are more useful when played one note at a time to provide an intro or bed, upon which other sounds can then be layered. Because you're not trying to emulate a real instrument, you can often use a single sample mapped across the whole keyboard, although in most situations you'll probably only ever use this type of sample over an octave or so. If you need the ability to sustain the sound indefinitely, you'll need to loop it, but with textural pads, selecting looping points isn't usually very difficult and a short crossfade at the loop edit point will avoid any audible glitching.

Practicalities Of Recording

You don't need an expensive mic to create some good samples, but a capacitor mic will produce the best results for bright sounds, although for kick-drum and tom sounds a dynamic mic is fine. My usual approach when producing this kind of sample is to set up the mic around a foot away from the object being struck and then change the mic position if this initial setting doesn't produce the desired result – for example, if you need more bottom end, a cardioid mic can be moved closer to the sound source to exploit the proximity effect. Longer mic distances are appropriate when you're miking something physically large, such as a garage door, but again experimentation is the key to success. The only criteria is whether the sound works or not –

the quality of the recording and how it was achieved is of secondary importance.

By recording to DAT, MiniDisc or directly into your computer before transferring the sounds to your sampler, you can experiment with recording levels and sort out the good sounds from the bad before you get down to sampling. If the attack of a sound is too slow, it can be either trimmed so that the first few milliseconds of the sample are discarded or layered with another sound. The kick drums of commercial records, for example, are often made up of a regular sampled sound layered with low-frequency sine-wave bursts from synths for added depth. Other sounds that work well alongside kick samples are things like finger snaps, claps, rimshots and other short sounds. The trick is to mix them low enough that they merge with the sample to create a new sound.

When it comes to processing, many short sounds benefit from have some reverb added to them, and of course you can use EQ just as you would for a regular recording. Once you start, the number of ways in which you can effect your samples is endless, and because you can amplify the sound to any level you like, the most insignificant event can form the basis of a huge-sounding sample – a snapping twig becomes a monster snare drum, a kitchen cleaver slammed into a cabbage gives you yet another kick drum, a length of scaffolding provides the basis for tuned industrial percussion and a cardboard box being hit can produce a whole range of kick and tom sounds. Bicycle spokes provide you with cheap marimbas, and don't even get me started on hitting the open end of a length of plastic waste pipe with a table-tennis bat! Even though you can buy CD-ROMs filled with hundreds of drum sounds, there's a lot of satisfaction in creating your own, and at least you know that they won't end up on anyone else's records. If you find that you like designing your own sample sounds, you should consider buying a portable MiniDisc recorder and taking it with you everywhere – you never know when you'll come across a unique sound, and if you don't have the means to capture it, it's lost forever.

Textural Sound Design

By combining the sounds from even a modest range of synthesisers and then using effects creatively, you can create complex pads and sound textures of your own. But don't limit your sound sources to synthesisers; a guitarist's wah-wah pedal stuck on the end of a fairly basic synth module can sound good, and many successful pads can be created by layering a more conventional pad sound over something evolving and strange. You'll find that synths like E-mu's Morpheus, the cheap-and-cheerful Kawai K1 and the ancient but still revered Korg Wavestation are good for generating the weirdness element, but you can also sample things like wind chimes, bamboo chimes and other 'real' sounds to layer beneath your pads.

Custom samples tend to rely heavily on effects, so a multi-effects unit of some sort is essential, and if you have one that includes a Vocoder then this will really open up your options. Those with access to a Lexicon PCM 70 or 80 or a Roger Linn AdrenaLinn will also find some interesting tuned-resonance effects, but cheap effects such as guitar pedals (particularly distortion boxes) are also useful.

I find that samples created entirely from synthetic sources have a certain electronic sameness to them, so I like to add natural sounds or those created using guitars and other instruments. Unpitched or vaguely pitched sounds, such as bamboo chimes and rainsticks, take on a quite different feel when you add effects and/or are pitch-shifted, while heavily treated electric guitar can often produce a more organic and evolving note than a synthesiser. There's also the human voice, which can be used as a Vocoder input or layered as it comes – for example, a sample choir patch sounds much more

basic Sampling

realistic and personal if you or a friendly vocalist can sing along to it. Multitrack a few new vocal layers, sample the result and you have your own choir sound.

Layering is also good for creating sounds that rely on several synths playing the same note at the same time, and the easiest way of doing this is by using a set of MIDI trigger notes to play the notes you need and then recording each synth part onto a separate audio track. This leaves you the option of octave-shifting, level-changing or even reversing any of the parts before you sample them, and you can also add different effects to each part if necessary. While this may require a lot of synths and effects to create, once it's been sampled you've only got to press one note to play it back.

A simple way of creating a shifting, evolving character to a sound is to layer two or more pad patches and then modulate their levels so that the balance changes constantly. Again, the automation features found in modern sequencers make this task very easy. By combining sounds that have some timbral similarities, such as string pads and choirs or voices and woodwind, you can create a slow-morphing effect where the sound mutates from being predominantly strings to predominantly choir and then back again. Where you're designing a stand-alone texture pad that you can play from one key, you can either make all the layers play the same note or create a chord. In the latter case, it's an idea to create both major and minor versions, and perhaps a root-plus-fifth version, which will give you more musical flexibility when you come to use the sound in a composition. You could do this by using keyboard splits so that you have one octave of major chords, one octave of minor chords and one octave of root-plus-fifth versions.

While I've mentioned using layers of bamboo chimes and bells in the background, you could also use sound of the natural environmental such as wind, rain, sea, running water, insect noises and birdsong, ideally treated with reverb, echo or ambience to give them a sense of space and distance.

Creative Guitar Samples

I've yet to hear guitar multisamples that sound convincing when played back, but for creating non-guitar-like, abstract sounds the electric guitar can be a wonderful source to sample – for example, if you can get your guitar to feed back on one note with very slow, very shallow vibrato, you'll find that it sits well with a layer of synthetic sound and adds a lot of interest. E-bows (electromagnetic bows that create

basic Sampling

indefinite sustain on single notes) make it very simple
to create controlled-feedback drones, and by changing
the tone controls on a guitar, amp or recording pre-
amp, you can get a whole range of sounds, from soft,
flute-like notes to harmonically rich, Eastern-sounding
effects. You could even add some filter sweeps with
a wah-wah pedal, while adding echo also creates a
richer sound.

Some other ways of coaxing sounds out of guitars are
bowing the strings with a violin bow, tapping each
string with a small screwdriver (which produces a nice
percussive dulcimer type of sound) and tuning the
guitar to an open chord (octaves or octave-and-fifth
combinations). Thumping the body of the guitar with
your hand can also set the strings ringing in an
interesting way, and with this trick you have the option
of keeping the thump or trimming it off when you come
to edit the sound.

Tuning down the whole guitar by four or five semitones
also produces an unusual timbre that samples well,
and of course you can use string scrapes, slides and
other incidental noises to add to your textural pads.
Always experiment with retuning samples, as a very
boring string scrape can sound like a piano being
demolished when it's dropped by a couple of octaves.

Effects And EQ

One of the easiest ways of treating a sample is to use EQ or the sampler's own filter to tame the harsh high end of a digital pad to make it sound more analogue. Guitar pre-amps with speaker simulators are also good for smoothing out sounds, and overdrive – where available – can make bland bass sounds much more aggressive.

In one of my own compositions, I layered eight different E-bow-sustained notes, playing root, octaves and fifths, then used a guitar pre-amp with a speaker simulator to smoothe off the rough edges before adding a combined chorus, stereo delay and long reverb. The eerie chordal drone that resulted was surprisingly rich and dynamic (although with this method it's also quite easy to achieve a seamless crossfade loop). From the layered notes, I was able to create a rich pad that could fit under most chord types, as only the root and fifth of the scale were used.

Unusual Effects

Some other effects, such as ring modulation, can also be used in conjunction with samplers. However, ring modulation has fairly limited musical uses because, while one note fed into it might sound wonderful, the next could sound completely discordant. But if you can get just one good sound out of it, you can sample it!

basic Sampling

A ring modulator is a device that processes two input signals to produce a new signal corresponding to the sum and difference of the input frequencies. If you put in two sine waves, two new pitches are produced, but if you use harmonically rich waveforms, you get a whole new spectrum of harmonics that aren't related to the original input in any musical way. Many ring modulators have built-in sine-wave oscillators that operate as second inputs, but if you have the option to modulate two entirely different sounds with each other, you have more chance of coming up with something fresh-sounding. The more complex the sounds are, the more dissonant the result, so it pays to keep the inputs harmonically simple. Vary the pitches of the two inputs relative to each other until you hear something you like and then record it for later sampling.

Percussion and bell sounds can also be used in a creative way. They are inherently atonal and so can be altered drastically to create new noises that bear no resemblance at all to the sound of the original instrument.

Meanwhile, effects boxes like the Lexicon PCM 80/81 include an interesting resonant-chord program where the pitches of multiple resonant delay lines can be 'played' from a MIDI keyboard. Any harmonically rich or percussive sound fed into the filters then takes on a chordal character that is dependant on the notes being played. With harmonically rich pad sounds processed in this way, some notes are subdued while others rise mysteriously out of the background whenever they coincide with the resonator pitches. With these devices, drum or percussion loops also make good source material. Again, record the results and sample the ones you like. Resonant programs are great tools for completely changing the character of commercial drum loops, and you'll find similar resonant programs in the Alesis Quadraverb and the Roger Linn AdrenaLinn guitar processor.

Vocoders Are Fun!

Vocoders process two signals so that one input imposes its spectral characteristics on the other. The usual example is modulating a keyboard pad using the human voice, but in the context of creating sounds to sample it's also possible to modulate drums using an harmonically rich keyboard pad or modulate one continuous sound with a completely different sound. Feeding in two synths playing the same part but with different sounds and different filter settings can also be quite productive, especially if you're looking for something a little unusual to add to a layered sound. The frequency spectrum of the modulator input is used to filter the carrier input, so both inputs are needed in order to produce an output.

Library Samples

While creating your own samples is to be encouraged, there are some sounds that are best left to the experts, and even the most adventurous professionals usually make use of CD-ROM library material. This requires a sampler either fitted with a CD-ROM drive or able to connect to an external drive, via SCSI, but I've found that some of the older Akai machines are very fussy about which SCSI CD-ROM drives they'll work with. This is something to be very wary of if you're buying used equipment, as is the high cost of the specialist memory boards used in some machines.

Sample-library CD-ROMs cost around ten times as much as music CD albums because they include a licence to use the samples that they contain. First of all, though, you need to be sure that these samples do what you need, so it's worth visiting a store that keeps a sample-CD jukebox so that you can hear what you're buying. You might also find that you can audition some samples via the internet, and some companies even allow you to download a few free samples as a means of promoting their libraries, so it's worth taking the time to investigate before you buy. There are also regular sample-library reviews in *Sound On Sound* magazine, with several years of back issues viewable online (free of charge for anything over six months old) at www.sospubs.co.uk.

Once you have access to CD-ROM libraries, you'll find that all of the hard work has already been done for you – the samples load up into neatly named programs, already looped and keygrouped, complete with appropriate envelope and modulation settings. Programs take a short while to load, but once you've booted one up in your sampler, it's just like playing a synth patch.

CD-ROM Compatibility

Akai, E-mu and Roland samplers are supported by a vast library of both in-house and third-party CD-ROMs, all of which use slightly different and mutually incompatible formats. Fortunately, most manufactures have built translation software into their instruments so that, for example, all of the later Akai machines will happily load both Roland and E-mu CD-ROMs. Clearly, this is good news for the user, but because every sampler has slightly different parameters and facilities (not to mention filter sounds), the degree of translation isn't always perfect. Often the only difference is a change in tonal quality, but you might find at times that you need to edit the programs to make them fully usable. When I used an Akai S2000, for example, I found that some of the samples created for earlier Akai machines load up in quirky ways, so a little manual tweaking might also be required.

basic Sampling

The mainstream hardware samplers have now been joined by a number of software equivalents, most of which can import and translate library material in some (but not all) of the other formats. Even though the Akai 5000 and 6000 machines have abandoned the sample format used by the earlier S3000 and similar machines, this format still prevails as the one standard format that most other samplers – both hardware and software – can import.

Commonly used software-sampler formats are SoundFont II (established by Creative Labs for their Soundblaster series of soundcards and beyond), Digidesign's SampleCell, Tascam's GigaSampler, Steinberg's Halion and Emagic's EXS24. These are by no means the only software samplers currently available, but at the time of writing they were the most widely used. New software samplers are appearing all the time, however, and they tend to support the most common of the competing formats first with others added later. As an example, the Emagic EXS24, which I now use for pretty much all of my sampling work, has its own EXS24 format and the ability to import Akai, Soft SampleCell and SoundFont II library material. There is also third-party sample-translation software available for converting almost any format to any other, so there's usually some way in which your computer can convert any type of sample into a format that your machine or soft sampler can use.

Sampling Without Samplers

While virtually all dance music is built around rhythm loops, often taken from sample CDs, you don't always have to use a sampler to take advantage of these sounds. There are specialist compositional programs available, such as Sonic Foundry's Acid or Ableton's Live, that are based around the manipulation of loops, although in many cases you need look no further than your sequencer.

All of the leading sequencer programs support audio recording and playback alongside MIDI, so if you want to use a musical phrase of a couple of bars of rhythm, you can load these straight into the audio tracks of your sequencer. In this case, the easiest format to handle is a sample-library audio CD, where you can use ripping software (such as Toast Audio Extractor on the Mac) to copy the audio files from CD directly to your hard drive, using the computer's own CD-ROM drive.

After importing a CD track, you'll be asked to name the audio file, which should be saved as a WAV, AIFF or SDII format file, in the case of Mac users, or a WAV file by PC users. Once safely on your hard drive, you can then import the file into your sequencer program and place it into an audio track. If necessary, use the Waveform Editor in your sequencer to trim the imported loop to exactly the right length before using it. CD sample libraries will always specify the tempo at which the recordings were made, so you'll need to either set your sequencer to the same tempo or use the time-/pitch-manipulation facilities in your sequencer to modify the loop length as required. Some audio software has the ability to work out the correct tempo based on the actual length of the imported loop, which can help when you aren't sure of the tempo of the material you're importing.

Once you've sorted out any tempo issues, it's best not to set the track's Loop parameter to allow the phrase to repeat indefinitely; instead, copy the phrase to all positions in the song where it's needed. No matter how many times you copy the section, it's always the original audio file that plays back, so no additional hard-drive space is used. As with using a regular sampler, triggering the phrase afresh each time avoids incurring any drift in sync, ensuring that there'll be no cumulative timing errors as the song progresses.

Using your sequencer to play back short musical phrases or loops at their original pitches is often easier than using a sampler to do the same job, and in the case of software samplers it also frees up CPU resources that would otherwise have been used to power a sampler plug-in. Because audio sequencer files are played directly from your hard drive, there's no sample-loading time and no maximum sample length. You can also make use of any audio-automation and -processing functions that are provided by your sequencer to make the loops sound more interesting.

It's easy to end up with too many samples, however, so organisation is important. It might be worth collecting together all of your most frequently used loops, phrases and sound effects and putting them onto categorised CD-Rs for easier access. And don't forget to keep back-ups of everything, because putting together a good sample library takes a lot of time.

6 TEMPO AND DRUM LOOPS

While there are numerous sample CDs and CD-ROMs full of useful and well-produced drum loops, there is a fundamental limitation in that a drum loop recorded at 120bpm (beats per minute) sounds right only when it's played back at the same tempo, or the pitch of the loop will move up or down in relation to its speed. It can be very frustrating when you check your drum-loop library and find exactly the rhythm you want but find that it's at 97bpm and your song is at 125bpm. Where the discrepancy is small, it's possible to use your keyboard's pitch-bend wheel to change the pitch – and hence the tempo of the sample – slightly, but you can only move most loops by a semitone or two before the change in sound quality is too great to be acceptable. Minor tempo adjustments can then be made by adjusting the pitch-bend value in the sequencer Edit list by small increments.

Alternatively, you can use your sampler or audio sequencer's time-stretching capabilities, but again the range over which tempo can be manipulated without the side-effects becoming noticeable is rather small. Of course, when you're working with musical styles in which side-effects are regarded as artistically desirable, there's no reason not to use time-stretching to make larger tempo changes. The necessary time-stretching percentage can be calculated from the original and desired loop tempos, as illustrated in the following example.

Assuming that a loop is running at 90bpm and you want to increase this to 120bpm, the percentage of time stretch is simply 90/120 x 100 per cent. Here, the length of the 90bpm sample needs to be made 75 per cent of its original length, thus the basic formula for percentage of time stretch needed is simply the original tempo divided by the destination tempo multiplied by 100 (per cent). Many samplers and software sample editors also make it possible for you to enter the start and end tempos directly, so you don't need to do any calculations yourself.

However, there are several viable alternatives to the above procedure that can give you much greater freedom to adjust the tempo of your material without sacrificing sound quality.

MIDI File Loops

The simplest solution to the same problem, and the one that offers the greatest flexibility when it comes to timing, is to either compose or buy commercial MIDI files of drum loops and then use these to control your own single-hit drum samples. This option is probably most helpful when you want to fit your own sounds to the rhythm of your material in order to avoid sounding like anyone else, but it makes it harder to create the kind of loop that depends on unusual percussion sounds or the use of effects. A lot of sound-design expertise goes into the production of the better commercial sample-loop libraries, and it can be difficult to get the same effect when using MIDI files to trigger your own samples. Even so, this shouldn't put you off trying; commercial MIDI file loop libraries are inexpensive compared to samples, and they're also easy to edit.

ReCycle And REX Files

Several years ago, Propellerhead Software teamed up with Steinberg to market their ReCycle program, a simple but effective software sample-editing program designed specifically for working with drum loops. Not only did ReCycle provide the means to trim and audition loops and to apply offline time-stretching, but it also came with a set of tools that enabled the user to slice up drum loops into their individual beats, which could then be triggered via MIDI to reproduce the original timing of the loop. This meant that the tempo of the loop would always follow the tempo of a sequencer song. Earlier versions of ReCycle worked only on mono

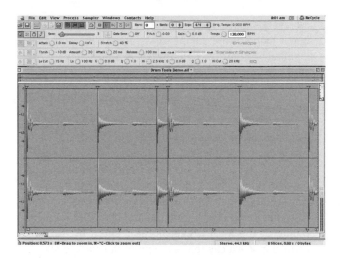

Figure 6.1: Main ReCycle screen with a drum loop marked for slicing

sound files, but ReCycle 2 – now marketed directly by Propellerhead – works with both mono and stereo files. Furthermore, many commercial rhythm-loop library samples are available in ReCycle format (REX file).

In ReCycle, a visual waveform display coupled with a variable-threshold system (similar in concept to the side-chain of a gate) for identifying the starts of beats makes dividing a bar or two of drum loop into slices relatively simple, and where a transient is missed, or one is marked where none exists, there's the option of manually adding or deleting slice points. Figure 6.1 shows the main ReCycle screen containing a drum loop marked for slicing.

It must be noted that slices aren't the same thing as individual drum sounds, as it all depends what's playing within any particular slice. For example, if the first beat of the bar comprises a kick, snare and hi-hat playing at the same time, that's the mix of sounds that the slice will contain. The next slice along may contain a hi-hat beat plus some reverb from the first slice. Because the timing of the MIDI trigger notes created by ReCycle corresponds exactly to the timing of the marked slices, playing back the loop at the original tempo will reconstruct the original loop exactly.

A ReCycle REX file saves all of the loop slices and their timing information in a format that can be read and used by any ReCycle-compatible program. A number of software samplers can also import REX files, placing the necessary MIDI trigger notes in the appropriate sequencer tracks automatically, although, because of the nature of drum loops, it's perfectly possible to use a REX-format drum loop directly from within a ReCycle-compatible sequencer track without the need to use a separate sampler.

With REX files, although the timing of the original slices is preserved, it's possible to quantise or change the tempo of slices just as you could with any MIDI part, but there are limitations – for instance, only one slice is allowed to play at a time, and so, if you increase the tempo, slices will be cut short to prevent them from overlapping. With modest tempo changes, this strategy works extremely well, but when it comes to slowing down REX files, gaps will be left between slices, which might or might not sound unnatural, depending on the nature of the loop. Adding reverb can sometimes disguise the gaps, but inevitably there's a limit to how much you can slow down a REX file before it starts to sound very unnatural. For this reason, it's often best to pick one that was created at a slightly lower tempo than you actually need, rather than one recorded at a higher tempo. I find that best results are achieved by moving not more than 20bpm or so from the original tempo, but this is very much a rule of thumb and much depends on the nature of the loop in question.

Groove Control

Groove Control files are conceptually similar to REX files, but they are used by only a limited number of sample-library developers – you can't buy software specifically to create Groove Control files. However, the simple way in which the sample slices and MIDI file data are supplied means that there's nothing stopping you achieving something similar by using available software tools, as long as you have the means to divide drum loops into slices. Commercial use of this format is controlled by Spectrasonics, the company that developed it.

A Groove Control library provides the necessary separate samples slices along with a separate 'trigger' MIDI file that can be copied and pasted into any sequencer track. (In most cases, this looks like a chromatic ramp of notes, with one note for each slice.) This means that any hardware or software sampler can be used to play back Groove Control libraries, whereas ReCycle files have the slicing information embedded within the audio file, so they can be used only by software that recognises and can import the REX format. Figure 6.2 shows the MIDI data associated with a typical Groove Control drum loop.

All Groove Control products are available in stereo and generally support the Akai S3000 format available on certain libraries. As most samplers can read the Akai S3000 format, there are few sampler users unable to take advantage of Groove Control libraries. However, you always need some type of sampler to use a Groove Control library, whereas REX files can be used directly from within those programs that support the REX

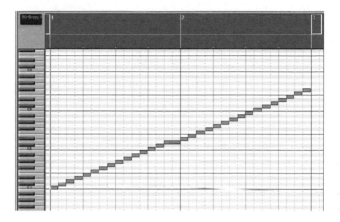

Figure 6.2: Groove Control MIDI file

format, such as Reason, Cubase and Logic Audio (from
version 5 upwards).

I've used a number of Groove Control libraries and
found their quality to be exceptionally good. In most
cases, the slices have been created long enough to
allow a substantial reduction in tempo before any gaps
become evident, so you can get them to sound natural
over quite a wide tempo range. Increasing tempo is
less of a problem, as the individual slices automatically
become shorter in proportion to the increase in tempo.

Tweaking

It's possible to modify both REX and Groove Control loops by changing the MIDI data that controls them. I'm a big fan of Groove Control libraries and find it trivially simple to change the feel of a pattern by using the Quantise and Swing functions on my sequencer to change the timing of the controlling MIDI data. Alternatively, where the MIDI file isn't quantised – for instance, where you want to retain the feel of the original performance – you can use the MIDI data to create a custom quantise template for syncing other MIDI-controlled parts of your song so that they sit more tightly with the drum groove. The newly created template generally appears as an extra option in your sequencer's Quantise window.

There's also the possibility that you can move the MIDI note data to trigger different slices, thereby changing what plays on certain beats of your loop. Meanwhile, beat levels can be changed by editing MIDI Velocity data and beats may even be removed altogether, although in my experience, if you want to get rid of, say, a snare-drum beat, it's best to replace this with a hi-hat slice or some other form of lightweight percussion in order to avoid incurring an obvious gap.

These simple editing techniques can be used to make a library sample less recognisable and also to customise rhythms to your specific needs, but if you're feeling more adventurous you can also layer different rhythmic elements on different sequencer tracks and then quantise them differently or delay one with respect to the other to create polyrhythms, hip-hop grooves and so on. This ability to experiment with the timing and construction of the controlling MIDI data means that both REX and Groove Control libraries open up far more creative possibilities than the more conventional 'use them as they come' samples.

APPENDIX
Common Cable Connections

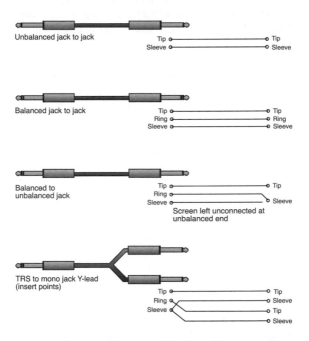

Unbalanced jack to jack

Tip o——————————o Tip
Sleeve o——————————o Sleeve

Balanced jack to jack

Tip o——————————o Tip
Ring o——————————o Ring
Sleeve o——————————o Sleeve

Balanced to
unbalanced jack

Tip o——————————o Tip
Ring o
Sleeve o——————————o Sleeve
Screen left unconnected at
unbalanced end

TRS to mono jack Y-lead
(insert points)

Tip o——————————o Tip
Ring o——————————o Sleeve
Sleeve o——————————o Tip
         ——————————o Sleeve

Appendix: Common Cable Connections

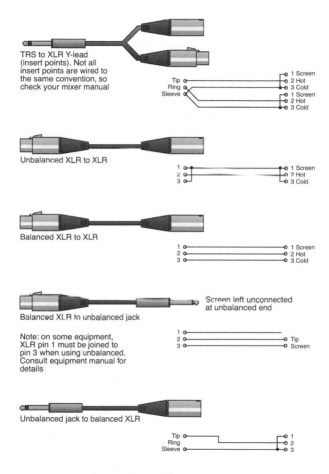

TRS to XLR Y-lead
(insert points). Not all
insert points are wired to
the same convention, so
check your mixer manual

Tip
Ring
Sleeve

1 Screen
2 Hot
3 Cold
1 Screen
2 Hot
3 Cold

Unbalanced XLR to XLR

1
2
3

1 Screen
2 Hot
3 Cold

Balanced XLR to XLR

1
2
3

1 Screen
2 Hot
3 Cold

Balanced XLR to unbalanced jack

Screen left unconnected
at unbalanced end

Note: on some equipment,
XLR pin 1 must be joined to
pin 3 when using unbalanced.
Consult equipment manual for
details

1
2
3

Tip
Screen

Unbalanced jack to balanced XLR

Tip
Ring
Sleeve

1
2
3

GLOSSARY

Active Sensing

System used to verify that a MIDI connection is working. This involves the source device sending short but frequent messages to the receiving device to reassure it that all is well. If these Active Sensing messages stop for any reason, the receiving device will recognise a fault condition and switch off all notes. Not all MIDI devices support active sensing.

ADSR

Envelope generator with Attack, Sustain, Decay and Release parameters. This is a simple type of envelope generator and was first used on early analogue synthesisers. This form of envelope generator continues to be popular on modern instruments. (See *Decay* for more details.)

Aftertouch

Means of generating a control signal based on how much pressure is applied to the keys of a MIDI keyboard. Most instruments that support this don't have independent pressure sensing for all keys, but instead detect overall pressure by means of a sensing strip running beneath the keys. Aftertouch may be used to control such functions as vibrato depth, filter brightness, loudness and so on.

Akai

One of the first companies to produce affordable samplers. It was therefore only natural that their sample-file format would become a standard for sample-library creators. Although other formats have emerged, the Akai S3000-compatible format remains a favourite with sample-library vendors, as many other hardware and software samplers can either read or convert from the Akai format.

Amplitude

Actual level of a signal, usually measured in volts.

Analogue

Term used to describe circuitry that uses a continually changing voltage or current to represent a signal. The origin of the term is that the electrical signal can be thought of as being analogous to the original signal.

Attenuate

To make lower in level.

Audio Frequency

Signals within the human audio range, nominally 20Hz–20kHz.

Automation

In the context of plug-in virtual instruments, many of the control movements you make can be recorded into the host sequencer as MIDI data, allowing the user to automate any desired parameters. Adjusting the cut-off frequency of a filter throughout a song is one of the more popular applications of virtual-instrument automation.

Balanced

Term used to describe a wiring system that uses two out-of-phase conductors and a common screen to reduce the effect of interference. In order for the process of balancing to be effective, the sending and the receiving device must have balanced output and input stages, respectively.

Bandpass Filter

Filter that removes or attenuates frequencies that fall above and below the threshold to which it is set, while frequencies within the band are emphasised. Bandpass filters are often used in synthesisers as tone-shaping elements.

Channel

In the context of MIDI, the term *channel* refers to one of 16 possible data channels over which MIDI data may be sent. The organisation of data by separate channels means that up to 16 different MIDI instruments or parts may be addressed over a single cable. In the context of mixing consoles, a channel is a single strip of controls relating to one input.

Cutoff Frequency

Frequency above or below which attenuation begins in a filter circuit.

Cycle

One complete vibration of a sound source or its electrical equivalent. One cycle per second is expressed as 1 Hertz (Hz).

Decay

Progressive reduction in amplitude of a sound or electrical signal over time. In the context of an ADSR envelope shaper, the Decay phase starts as soon as the Attack phase has reached its maximum level. In the Decay phase, the signal level drops until it reaches the Sustain level set by the user. The signal then remains at this level until the key is released, at which point the Release phase is entered.

Digital

Term used to describe an electronic system that represents data and signals in the form of codes comprising 1s and os.

DMA

Abbreviation of Direct Memory Access, part of a computer operating system that allows peripheral devices to communicate directly with the computer memory without going via the central processor (CPU).

Envelope

Mathematical model describing the way in which the level of a sound or signal varies over time.

Envelope Generator

Circuit capable of generating a control signal representing the envelope of a desired sound. This may then be used to control the level of an oscillator or other sound source, although envelopes may also be used to control filter or modulation settings. The most common example of an envelope generator is an ADSR generator.

Event

In MIDI terms, an event is a single unit of MIDI data, such as a note being turned on or off, a piece of controller information, a Program Change message and so on.

File

Meaningful list of data stored in digital form. A Standard MIDI File is a specific type of file designed to allow sequence information to be interchanged between different types of sequencer.

Filter

Type of powerful tone-shaping network used in synthesisers to create tonal sweeps and wah-wah effects. The term *filter* may also be found in some MIDI sequencers where there is provision to exclude or filter out certain types of MIDI data – for example, Aftertouch data.

Gate

Electrical signal that is generated whenever a key is depressed on an electronic keyboard. This action triggers envelope generators and other events that need to be synchronised to key action. In the case of MIDI keyboards, the gate signal is converted into Note On and Note Off messages.

General MIDI

Addition to the basic MIDI specification designed to

assure a minimum level of compatibility when playing back General MIDI-format song files. The specification covers type and program number of sounds, minimum polyphony and multitimbrality levels, response to controller information and other criteria.

GigaSampler
Software sampler produced by Tascam that streams audio from a hard disk in order to facilitate the playback of large sample libraries.

GM Reset
Universal Sysex command that activates the General MIDI mode on a GM instrument. The same command also sets all controllers to their default values and switches off any notes still playing by means of an All Notes Off message.

Groove Control
File format developed by Spectrasonics for the preparation of loop-based sample libraries, allowing variable tempo playback. The concept is not dissimilar to REX files, except that Groove Control samples can be played back on any sequencer, as the necessary MIDI files (which are needed to drive the sample slices) are provided separately rather than integrated into the sample file, as is the case with REX files. However,

whereas REX files can be created by anyone owning a copy of ReCycle, Groove Control is purely a library format, not a system by which users can create their own Groove Control loops.

GS
Roland's own extension to the General MIDI protocol.

High-Pass Filter
Filter that attenuates frequencies falling below its cut-off frequency threshold.

IRQ
Abbreviation of Interrupt Request. Part of the operating system of a computer that allows a connected device to request attention from the processor in order to transfer data to it or from it.

LFO
Abbreviation of Low-Frequency Oscillator, which is used as a modulation source, usually below 20Hz. The most common LFO waveshape is the sine wave, although most give the choice of sine, square, triangular and sawtooth waveforms.

Local On/Off
Function that allows a keyboard and the sound-

generating section of a keyboard synthesiser to be used
independently of each other.

Low-Pass Filter
Filter that attenuates frequencies falling above its cut-
off frequency.

LSB
Abbreviation of Least Significant Byte. If a piece of data
has to be conveyed as two bytes, one byte represents
high-value numbers and the other low-value numbers,
much in the same way as tens and units function in
the decimal system. The high value, or most significant,
part of the message is called the Most Significant Byte
(MSB).

MIDI
Musical Instrument Digital Interface.

MIDI Bank Change
Controller message used to select alternate banks of
MIDI programs where access to more than 128 programs
is required.

MIDI Control Change
Also known as MIDI controllers or controller data, these
messages contain positional information relating to

performance controls such as wheels, pedals, switches and other devices. This information can then be used to control such functions as vibrato depth, brightness, portamento, effects levels and many other parameters.

MIDI controller

Term used to describe the physical interface by means of which a musician plays a MIDI synthesiser or other sound generator. Examples of controllers are keyboards, drum pads and wind synths.

(Standard) MIDI File

See *File*.

MIDI Implementation Chart

Chart usually found in the backs of MIDI product manuals that provides information concerning which MIDI features are supported. Supported features are marked with a o while unsupported feature are marked with an X. Additional information may also be provided, such as the exact form of MIDI Bank Change messages.

MIDI In

Socket on a MIDI device that receives information from a master controller or from the MIDI Thru socket of a slave unit.

MIDI Merge
Device or sequencer function that enables two or more streams of MIDI data to be combined.

MIDI Mode
MIDI information can be interpreted by a receiving MIDI instrument in a number of ways, the most common being polyphonically on a single MIDI channel (Poly/Omni Off mode). Omni mode enables a MIDI instrument to play all incoming data, regardless of the channel on which it's sent.

MIDI Module
Sound-generating device with no integral keyboard.

MIDI Note Number
Every key on a MIDI keyboard has its own note number, ranging from 0 to 127, where 60 represents middle C. Some systems use C3 as middle C while others use C4.

MIDI Note Off
MIDI message sent when a key is released.

MIDI Note On
MIDI message sent when a note is played (ie a key is pressed).

MIDI Out
MIDI connector used to send data from a master device to the MIDI In of a connected slave device.

MIDI Port
MIDI connections of a MIDI-compatible device. A multiport, in the context of a MIDI interface, is a device with multiple MIDI output sockets, each capable of carrying data relating to a different set of 16 MIDI channels. Multiports are the only means of exceeding the limitations imposed by 16 MIDI channels.

MIDI Program Change
Type of MIDI message used to change sound patches on a remote module or the effects patch on a MIDI effects unit.

MIDI Splitter
Alternative term for MIDI Thru box.

MIDI Sync
Description of the synchronisation systems available to MIDI users: MIDI Clock and MTC (MIDI Time Code).

MIDI Thru
Socket on a slave unit used to feed the MIDI In socket of the next unit in line.

MIDI Thru Box

Device that splits the MIDI Out signal of a master instrument or sequencer in order to avoid daisy-chaining. Powered circuitry is used to buffer the outputs to prevent problems occurring when many pieces of equipment are driven from a single MIDI output.

Multitimbral Module

MIDI sound source capable of producing several different sounds at the same time and controlled on different MIDI channels.

Non-Registered Parameter Number

Addition to the basic MIDI spec that allows controllers 98 and 99 to be used to govern non-standard parameters relating to particular models of synthesiser. This is an alternative to using Sysex (system-exclusive) data to achieve the same ends. NRPNs tend to be used mainly by Yamaha and Roland instruments.

Oscillator

Circuit designed to generate a periodic electrical waveform. In a sampler, the recorded audio sample takes the place of the tone-oscillator waveform.

Patch

Alternative term for *program*, referring to a single

programmed sound within a synth that can be called up using Program Change commands. MIDI effects units and samplers also have patches.

Pitch Bend

Special control message designed specifically to produce a change in pitch in response to the movement of a pitch-bend wheel or lever. Pitch-bend data can be recorded and edited, just like any other MIDI controller data, even though it isn't part of the Controller messages group.

Plug-in

Software designed to work from within a host application to provide extra features. Most virtual instruments, including software samplers, work as plug-ins.

Polyphony

Term used to describe the ability of an instrument to play two or more notes simultaneously. An instrument that can play only one note at a time is described as *monophonic*.

Portamento

Gliding effect that allows a sound to change pitch at a gradual rate when a new key is pressed or a new MIDI note is sent.

Pressure
Alternative term for *aftertouch*.

Pulse Wave
Similar to a square wave but non-symmetrical. Pulse waves sound brighter and thinner than square waves, making them useful in the synthesis of reed instruments. The timbre changes according to the mark/space ratio of the waveform.

Pulse-Width Modulation
Means of modulating the duty cycle (mark/space ratio) of a pulse wave, thus changing the timbre of the basic tone. LFO modulation of pulse width can be used to produce a pseudo-chorus effect. Although pulse-width modulation can't be applied to samples, a similar effect can be created by slightly detuning two similar sounds.

Q
Alternative term for *equalisation*, a measure of the resonant properties of a filter. The higher the Q value, the more resonant the filter and the narrower the range of frequencies that are allowed to pass.

Quantise
Means of moving notes recorded in a MIDI sequencer so that they line up with user-defined subdivisions of

a musical bar – for example, 16th notes. The facility may be used to correct timing errors, but over-quantisation can remove the human feel from a performance.

RAM

Abbreviation of Random Access Memory, a type of memory used by computers for the temporary storage of programs and data. All RAM data is lost when the power is turned off, so work needs to be saved to disk if it is not to be lost at the end of each session.

ReCycle

Sample-editing program that slices loops into beat-length segments which can then be played back over a range of tempos under control of a special MIDI file responsible for triggering the slices in sequence. A ReCycle file is saved in the REX file format, which is supported by a number of third-party sequencers and software samplers.

Release

Term used to describe the rate at which a signal amplitude decays once a key has been released.

Resonance

Characteristic of a filter that allows it to pass selectively a narrow range of frequencies. (See *Q*.)

Ring Modulator

Device that accepts and processes two input signals in a particular way. The output signal does not contain any of the original input signal but instead comprises new frequencies based on the sum and difference of the input signals' frequency components.

ROM

Abbreviation of Read Only Memory, a permanent, or non-volatile, type of memory containing data that can't be changed. Operating systems are often stored on ROM as the memory remains intact when the power is removed.

E-PROM

Abbreviation of Erasable Programmable Read-Only Memory and similar to ROM, but on E-PROM chips the stored information can be erased and replaced with the use of special equipment.

Sample And Hold

Usually refers to a feature whereby random values are generated at regular intervals and then used to control another function, such as pitch or filter frequency. Sample-and-hold circuits were also used in analogue synthesisers to 'remember' the notes being played after the keys had been released.

Sample

The term *sample* has two common meanings in electronic music. Audio is sampled during the analogue-to-digital conversion process, in which case a sample is a single 'snapshot' of the audio-signal level. Upwards of 40,000 samples are required each second to record audio to a sufficiently high standard.

The other meaning of the term, which is relevant to samplers, is a short section of audio – such as an instrument note, a drum rhythm or a vocal phrase – that a sampler can load and play back.

Sawtooth

Waveform that resembles the teeth of a saw, containing only even harmonics.

SCSI

Abbreviation of Small Computer System Interface, an interfacing system for using hard drives, scanners, CD-ROM drives and similar peripherals with a computer. Each SCSI device has its own ID number, and no two SCSI devices in the same chain must be set to the same number. The last SCSI device in the chain should be terminated, either via an internal terminator (where provided) or via a plug-in terminator fitted to a free SCSI socket. Many hardware sequencers use SCSI to save sample data to an external hard drive or to connect to a computer editing program.

Sequencer
Device used for the recording and replaying of MIDI data, usually in a multitrack format, allowing complex compositions to be built up a part at a time.

Sine Wave
Pure-tone waveform with no harmonics.

Slave
MIDI device under the control of a master device, such as a sequencer or master keyboard.

Square Wave
Symmetrical rectangular waveform containing a series of odd harmonics.

Streaming
Delivery of audio directly from a hard drive rather than from RAM. A number of software samplers are able to stream audio from a computer's hard drive, the advantage of this being that longer samples can be used than can be accommodated in RAM.

Subtractive Synthesis

Process of creating a new sound by filtering and shaping a raw, harmonically complex waveform. Most samplers function as subtractive synthesisers, where the sampled waveform is further processed by filters and envelope shapers.

Timbre
Tonal 'colour' of a sound.

Tremolo
Modulation of the amplitude of a sound using an LFO.

Triangle Wave
Symmetrical, triangle-shaped wave containing only odd harmonics, but with a lower harmonic content than a square wave.

Velocity
Term used to describe the rate at which a key is depressed. Velocity data may be used to control loudness (to simulate the response of instruments such as pianos) or other parameters on modern synthesisers.

Vibrato
Pitch modulation using an LFO to modulate a tone oscillator or the frequency of a sample.

Virtual Instrument
Software-based musical instrument.

Voice
Single musical note of an instrument. A 16-voice instrument is one that is capable of playing 16 simultaneous notes.

VST
Abbreviation of Virtual Studio Technology, Steinberg's format for plug-in effects and virtual instruments.

Waveform
Graphic representation of the way in which a sound wave or electrical wave varies over time.

XG
Yamaha's alternative to Roland's GS system for enhancing the General MIDI protocol so as to provide additional banks of patches and further editing facilities.